Antisemitism During the French Second Empire

American University Studies

Series IX
History
Vol. 100

PETER LANG
New York · San Francisco · Bern
Frankfurt am Main · Paris · London

Natalie Isser

Antisemitism During the French Second Empire

PETER LANG
New York · San Francisco · Bern
Frankfurt am Main · Paris · London

Library of Congress Cataloging-in-Publication Data

Isser, Natalie
    Antisemitism during the French Second Empire /
Natalie Isser.
      p. cm. — (American university studies. Series IX,
History ; 100)
      Includes bibliographical references and index.
      1. Antisemitism—France—History—19th century.
2. France—Politics and government—1852-1870. 3. Jews—
France—History—19th century. 4. France—Ethnic
relations. I. Title. II. Series: American university
studies. Series IX, History ; vol. 100.
DS146.F8187   1991   944'.004924—dc20   90-21535
ISBN 0-8204-1454-9   CIP
ISSN 0740-0462

CIP-Titelaufnahme der Deutschen Bibliothek

Isser, Natalie
Antisemitism during the French Second Empire / Natalie
Isser.—New York; Bern; Frankfurt am Main; Paris:
Lang, 1991
  (American university studies : Ser. 9, History ;
Vol. 100)
  ISBN 0-8204-1454-9
NE: American university studies / 09

Acknowledgments

It is impossible to write and engage in scholarly pursuits without the aid, encouragement, and advice of innumerable colleagues, friends, and family.

I extend my heartfelt appreciation to Lita L. Schwartz for her critical appraisals and for her lively insights into psychology. Claire Hirshfield also contributed significant editorial comment and advice. Translations were graciously provided by Mr. Vincent Virgulti. Mrs. Margaret Taylor aided in the typing and Dr. Tom Warms and Terrie Smith aided in the final preparation of the manuscript.

I owe a special debt of gratitude to all the unnamed and unknown staffs of the various archives and libraries that I visited. They included the Archives Nationales and the Bibliotheque Nationale (Paris), British Museum and Public Record Office (London), the Central Zionist Archives, and Ecce Homo (Jerusalem), the Library of Congress, the New York Public Library, Leo Baecke Institute, Widener Library (Harvard) and the Van Pelt Library (University of Pennsylvania) as well as others. I am especially thankful for the efforts of the personnel of the library of the Ogontz Campus, Penn State University, especially Mrs. Dita Schmidt, Hazel McCutcheon, and Dorothy Sharpe. These gentle ladies were patient, persevering and kind.

A large part of my work was made possible by the generous financial assistance of The Pennsylvania State University Commonwealth Campus Scholarly Fund. A part of this book has been published as articles in the journals *Revue des Etudes Juives* and *Adolescence*.

Finally, my husband Leonard provided the support, companionship and humor essential for the completion of this work.

N. I.

Ogontz Campus
Pennsylvania State University

Table of Contents

Preface

Antisemitism, defined as hostility to and dislike of Jews, has had a nefarious continuity in the evolving social and political institutions of western civilization. There are no weights and measures to define its parameters. The expression of prejudice can be established by barriers to assimilation or, as some have noted, by the denial of the maintenance and legitimacy of the ethnic religious community. The definition of anti-semitism can and does take many shapes and forms within a context best described as anti-Jewish feeling. It can encompass those whose reasoning employs mildly prejudicial stereotypes, or it can be expressed in terms of a group's self-interest, or in institutional assertions of fixed and rigid attitudes about Jews, or finally, through an overt hostility acted out in violent deeds.

Antisemitism has given rise to a variety of images, ideas, and themes, which have penetrated into many cultures and nations. For instance, in ancient times, Jews were perceived as a stiff–necked, stubborn people who were reviled because they clung to their ethnic identity and their own God. In the middle ages, the Christian Church portrayed the Jews as Satan's disciples or as infidels, subjecting them to hatred and scorn. Modern societies have interjected racial theories and social Darwinism.

Throughout history, social slights, pejorative comments, snobbery, as well as legal restrictions and economic barriers, have formed an integral part of the victimization of the Jews. They have been condemned for being devout, and equally criticized for not following the precepts of their faith. They have been hated because they were poor, and loathed when they were rich and successful. They have been condemned because they were international bankers and capitalists, but equally castigated as being the instigators of international socialism and communism. They have been accused of assimilating into the mainstream culture, and also condemned because they were too "clannish." In other words, Jews were the source of whatever evil the majority wished to impute to them. Sometimes the victims have been indicted as the cause of their own victimization.

Cogent, rational explanations for this behavior also varied. Politically Jews provided a satisfying scapegoat for those seeking power. They were a convenient foil upon whom the deprived could wreak anger. Psychoanalysts, on the other hand, perceived the conflict as an expression of unconscious guilt in man's eternal struggle with his "father": antisemitism representing the repressed feelings in generational opposition of the young faith to the "parent" religion. Social psychologists identified Jews as the perennial "outsider." Since most societies denied the concept of cultural pluralism, Jewish religious and ethnic community was regarded as dangerous. Some socialists used economic stereotypes to arouse enthusiasm for their cause among the poor. A few philosophers and theologians ascribed hostility to Judaism as a part of the teachings of Christianity. They claimed religious indoctrination was able to perpetuate traditional animosities which justified mistreatment of the Jews. In contrast, there were those who wished to diminish the role of organized Christianity, and the most effective weapon in that struggle was to attack Judaism.

More significantly, antisemitism (whatever the cause or causes) revealed the nature of the social pathologies of the host society. Indeed, the similarity between nations indicated the common experience of the discontinuities of the modernization process. Yet differences in the manifestations of hate illustrated the variety of the crises of cultural despair.

The tragic denouement of the Jews in the Holocaust has inspired many scholars to investigate, once again, the nature and historical development of European antisemitism. The aim of this study is to examine and define the peculiar characteristics of French antisemitism as it emerged in the nineteenth century. Antisemitism was a persistent theme throughout French history, but historians and commentators developed not only differing, but contradictory views of this sentiment. Eugen Weber characterized antithetical feelings toward Jews as a peripheral and almost insignificant feature of French culture. Zeldin observed that the Jewish population of France was so small that most Frenchmen had no contact with Jews, and therefore antisemitism never became widespread; it only become a problem at the end of the nineteenth century. In contrast other historians have excoriated French behavior claiming French antisemitism was a major force in French life.[1] These existing divergent opinions should not be surprising, for they reflect the dichotomies inherent in French development. The variety of interpretations reflect both the realities and ambiguities of French culture. The purpose of this study was to discover the origin of these divergences and the factors in French life that produced such contradictions. The Second French Empire is the period best suited for such an analysis because that time period provided the bridge between the emancipation of the Jews and the development of modern antisemitism. Therefore, this book has focused upon the development of antisemitism from 1850 to 1870, in order to provide a better assessment of the complexities of French antisemitism.

[1] For a variety of interpretations see Frances Malino and Bernard Wasserstein (eds.), *The Jews in Modern France* (Hanover, London: Univ. of New England Press, 1985).

Antisemitism During the French Second Empire

Chapter I

Introduction

The Second Empire was a period which encompassed rapid change as France underwent extensive modernization, characterized by the development of railroads, innovations in banking and the growth of commerce, mining, and manufacturing. These factors affected the relationship between social classes; they led to the growth of cities, to increasingly new avenues of opportunities for women, and more significantly to a shift of political forces as the former notables' influence and prestige was replaced by a more professional government bureaucracy. Napoleon III, by 1852, had firmly established the Empire and had consolidated his power by the use of authoritarian measures. However, the exigencies of economic and social change led to the erosion of repression and to the creation of more liberal institutions, beginning in the 1860s.

Intellectual currents were also stimulated by continuing economic prosperity and growth. The increased respect for science and technology inspired renewed interest in education, which in turn led to impassioned debates on the role of the church in French schools. The railroads and the expansion of industry stimulated both trade and travel among the middle classes, resulting in a greater worldliness caused by the intermingling of cultures. Indeed, this cosmopolitanism was encouraged by the court itself. The Emperor welcomed famous artists from abroad to perform, and then encouraged them to remain in Paris to add to the vitality and intellectual "esprit" of the capital. The most notable and popular of these figures were the painter Winterhalter and composers Meyerbeer and Offenbach. New elements also appeared in literature as writers turned to realism, and romanticism gradually lost its appeal. Painting and the plastic arts also developed the same tendencies. Urban renewal, increased wealth, and an everspreading literacy created a more politically sophisticated populace, a development abetted by the creation of the mass press and the more rapid transmission of the news.

Hence, modernization brought change to every facet of French life, creating dislocations, social antagonisms, and generational conflicts. These upheavals, accompanied by rapidity of change, also brought in their wake anomie, alienation, and apprehension. Yet, on the surface, the society of the Empire seemed quiescent: the epitome of a bourgeois materialistic civilization. However, underneath this ostensibly stable society lurked conflicts created by rapid innovation, and emotions of despair and nostalgia for past traditional values. These underlying hostilities were characterized by enduring schisms among the working classes and bourgeoisie which would again emerge in the tragic events of 1871.[1] The Church, too, faced new challenges posed by the impact of industrial life and expanded urbanism. Religious behavior was affected by the enormous growth of the secular spirit reflected by reduced attendance at Sunday mass and the lessening participation in the Easter Communion, especially in the cities. But, at the same time (as in the present), many felt threatened by what they perceived was a decline in public morality and a weakening of traditional values. The French responded to modernization, not by new millenarian movements or outbursts of religiosity as in other societies,[2] but rather by the growth of a variety of miracle cults and prophetic movements: the most famous being Lourdes.[3] These groups, especially the confraternities, helped to perpetuate a conservative religious nationalism that was eventually to become the focus for antisemitism.

The development of social pathology, one of the results of modernization, was often expressed in a more or less virulent fashion by persecution or by pejorative disdain of traditional minorities in many communities. In France, the groups most vulnerable to such harassment were Protestants, Jews, and Freemasons. Yet historians, often relying upon contemporary observations, felt that antisemitism was not a significant force during the Second Empire, because prejudice was not overtly practiced. Many significant works on antisemitism by such notable authors as Byrnes, Marrus, Pierrard either do not mention the Second Empire, or at best, place the major emphasis on the latter half of the nineteenth century.[4] Nevertheless, the old fears, superstitions, and stereotypes were submerged, and they resurfaced during the political and emotional agonies caused by the Franco-Prussian War, the Commune, and the strains of the Third Republic.[5] Therefore, the Second Empire as well as the preceding Orleans Monarchy was regarded by scholars as an era of "good feelings" toward Jews. There were few major crises, at least none that matched the virulence of the later Dreyfus Affair. Thus as one scholar noted:

In France, a seemingly firm stabilization of emancipation, entailing full legal equality, was reached
under the Bourbon and Orleans monarchies and continued under the Second Empire of Napoleon III.
. . . There, then, was a seemingly sudden rise of
antisemitism . . . which culminated in the Panama
Scandal and above all in the Dreyfus Affair.[6]

That sentiment was noted by another eminent scholar who said "prior to the
Dreyfus case antisemitism was a comparatively minor problem in France."[7]
Contemporary observers agreed that Jews seemed to enjoy complete protection and liberty during the eighteen years of Napoleon III.   One politician
cogently expressed this view:

If I can make an allusion to those political battles,
in which I played a modest role, I could not be
accused of any partiality for the regime that emerged from the Coup d'État of 2 December but I
must admit that there was no trace in the history
of the Second Empire of any antisemitism. I must
add that the Second Empire, on several occasions,
was the champion of freedom of religion in Europe
and the protector of the persecuted. . . . [8]

British Jews seeking full emancipation saw in France the fulfillment of their
own political aspirations and sought the same rights. One observer wrote:

. . . We are, therefore, happy to state that Jewish affairs in Paris and throughout France are in a very
flourishing condition; it proves clearly that liberty,
civil rights, and Jewish religion can be harmonized,
and that it is a false reproach that the Jew cannot be
a good citizen.[9]

The historical legacy that created such a political climate for the Jews
of the Second Empire rested in the developments of the Revolution of 1789.
At the time of the upheavals the Jewish community numbered about
40,000, comprising 1% of the population; so minute in size that many
Frenchmen had never had contact with Jews at all.   Not only were Jews
numerically small, but their community was neither cohesive, nor ethnically unified; its members did not even speak the same language.   There

4

were three major groups: those who lived in Avignon and Southern France called Comitadin, those of Portuguese descent who lived in Southwestern France (around Bordeaux), and those who lived in Alsace-Lorraine. The Comitadin were the oldest group in France, residing in the Papal enclaves or in Southern cities. The Portuguese and Spanish Jews (who lived in Paris) spoke Ladino, and they practiced Sephardic religious rites. These two groups had already begun to assimilate into French life; secularization slowly proceeded as laymen were gradually assuming leadership in their congregations and their communities.[10]

The third group, and by far the largest, was concentrated in Alsace-Lorraine. They spoke Yiddish, and they differed from other French Jews because their customs and religious rites were Germanic or Ashkenazic. Their community life was more insular and isolated. They were also much poorer; and a large number of them were engaged in usury. Indeed, Jews provided the only source of credit for the impoverished Alsatian peasants who needed funds for horses or agricultural supplies.[11] The social and religious barriers to integration were far greater than in the rest of France.

The French revolutionaries, believing in the universality of the natural law, and developing the concept of the modern nation-state, granted full emancipation to the Jews, meaning that Jews were to be regarded as citizens with full civil and political rights. They could enjoy freedom of religion and, for the first time, they had complete freedom of movement. A result of this new freedom was that Jews began a continuing migration to the cities.

Napoleon Bonaparte continued the revolutionary tradition of religious toleration, but as a more authoritarian ruler, he mandated that his government supervise all religious institutions, Protestant and Catholic as well. He, therefore, established regulations that molded the life of Jews (and also influenced other western Jewish European communities) throughout the nineteenth and twentieth centuries. Napoleon perceived Jews not only as a separate religious group, but also as a distinct culture or race which he was determined to assimilate into French life. Indeed, that was also the view of the French liberals who demanded cultural assimilation, a point of view often supported by "Court Jews" themselves.[12] Emancipation thus carried a price, for cultural pluralism was eschewed. Many even desired an end to religious diversity by entertaining the hope that eventually the Jewish community would be absorbed through conversion.[13]

To that end, Napoleon established the Great Sanhedrin whose major task was to adjust Judaic practices to the exigencies of French political life.

The Sanhedrin agreed to civil marriage, the abolition of polygamy (not practiced at the time), and service in the military. To make state regulation easier, Jews were grouped in territorial units headed by a consistory of laymen who would direct religious affairs. Rabbis would be elected by consistories.[14] Napoleonic decrees, aiming for total assimilation, insisted that these Jews take surnames. Napoleon was also cognizant of the social and economic tensions that existed in Alsace, and hoped to both reduce antagonisms and eradicate the local cultural autonomy of the Jewish communities. Therefore, he created special laws regulating usury and supervising Jewish conduct. The rights of Jews in Northern and Eastern France were circumscribed by the so-called "infamous" decree of 1808, which was, however, "to be annulled after ten years if they (the Jews) behaved well."[15] Historians disagree on whether these decrees were antisemitic or whether they responded to social necessity.[16] Although Napoleon was defeated in 1815, the consistorial system was not only maintained, but it also consolidated its influence. The infamous decree of 1808 was not renewed in 1818 and the Central Consistory was recognized as an official body by the king. During the Orleans Monarchy in 1831, the Jewish religion was granted financial parity with other French religions when rabbis' salaries were paid by the state. In 1846, the last obstacle to compete equality was destroyed when the special oath, *more judaica*, was finally abolished.

French Jews assimilated culturally, becoming Frenchmen who worshipped in the Jewish faith. They spoke French, and their children attended French schools. Their leaders preached full integration into French society and engagement in French cultural development. Despite occasional social snobbery and some prejudicial comments in public places, some Jews had achieved equality and prominence in banking, in business enterprises, and in the arts and the professions. Some Jews had been accepted by the upper classes, and even in high society. Government administrative officials indicated that Jews were judged as good French citizens if they exhibited the following qualities: sobriety, adherence to the maintenance of good order, less overt desire for wealth, and less conformity to their religion and its practices. However, those Jews who remained orthodox, poor, or engaged in the second hand trade or peddling (mostly those who resided in Alsace) were subjected to the older Christian prejudices. These stereotypes persisted, and were reflected in the larger society, as the prefects derided "ethnic" Jews or those who were fanatically devoted to "Torah." They felt that religious Jews were less able to achieve economic mobility or for that matter, "to behave well." In the prefect's eyes only an assimilated Jew was a "good" Jew.[17]

Hence, the Jew often reacted by adopting the beliefs of the majority, and lessened the religious dimension of his life as he actively pursued his newly available national identity. There were symptoms, nevertheless, that indicated that these communities remained cohesive and identifiable. For example, the Jews tended to reside in more urban-oriented areas, concentrated in villages and cities, and they continued to focus on certain businesses, trades, and professions. Acculturation took place in Alsace-Lorraine at a much slower pace because Jews had fewer economic opportunities, and because they had to learn French as well.

Their children, however, were often tempted by the seduction and promise of the majority religion and the social gains promised through conversion. Further, the Jewish community itself was a direct target of both Catholic and Protestant missionary activity. There were some famous conversions: David Drach, son-in-law of the great Rabbi Deutz; the notable Father Libermann, and Alphonse and Theodore Ratisbonne, grandsons of Cerf Berr, prominent Jewish leader in Strasbourg, and sons of the president of the Consistory of the Lower Rhine. Drach and the Ratisbonnes were famous for their efforts to convert their fellow Jews. Even the children of the eminent jurist Adolph Crémieux were baptized by their mother without their father's knowledge.[18] Among the forces leading to such conversion might be the quest for social advantages, the satisfaction of psychological needs, or perhaps the logical consequence of assimilation, satisfying aspirations of becoming *totally* French.[19] These active attempts to convert Jewish young people alarmed their elders who worried about the future of the Jewish community.[20] Concern was expressed in the Jewish press in England and in France over the efforts of the "conversionists."[21] Intermarriage added to the problems.

Even more insidious and more widespread, and an enemy to other faiths as well, was the prevailing secularism which was eagerly embraced by innumerable Jews. This further vitiated the intellectual and religious vigor of some Jewish community institutions and Jewish intellectual development. Jews outside of Alsace-Lorraine rapidly assimilated into the mainstream French culture. Many young people recoiled from actual conversion because of a personal sense of honor and loyalty to their family, and instead became deists, agnostics, or in a few cases Saint-Simonian socialists. They refrained from active religious observance, and no longer spoke or read Hebrew. Notable figures such as the actress Rachel, the composer Meyerbeer, the Millauds, Pereires, and d'Eichthal were "marginal" figures of French society. Accepted in French life as Jews, they had only a nominal affiliation with their own community, and yet had not fully integrated into the "other."[22] As Jews assimilated culturally, they became Frenchmen who worshiped in the Jewish faith. They were the lay leaders of Jewish charitable organizations and of the Consistories as well. Even in Alsace, where acculturation was more rare, the Ratisbonnes, leaders of the Strasbourg Consistory, were non-observant Jews.

To counter these centrifugal influences of missionaries, secularism, and intermarriage, Jewish leaders founded their own schools (with government subsidy) to teach Jewish children some principles of Jewish religion, vocational trades, and those skills needed to enter into French society. However, these schools were aimed primarily for poor families and their children. The middle classes, especially the wealthier bourgeois, sent their children to public schools and when possible, to lycees and universities. For many years Jews, and especially professors, had been excluded from the more advanced courses. During the Revolution of 1848 and after, Catholic pressure exerted by some bishops prevented the appointment of Jewish teachers and professors in several schools. As late as 1852, Jewish and Protestant students were still not accepted in the École Normale, and there were other scattered cases of denial to higher educational institutions. Nevertheless, wealthier Jews preferred public schools for their children. Jewish schools, on the other hand, were not heavily funded, their teachers were paid poorly, and they were not strongly supportive of religious instruction.   Hebrew was generally neglected and the French language was emphasized, especially in Alsace, where Yiddish was still the spoken language.[23]

Just as Jewish educational institutions adapted to helping poorer Jewish youth acculturate, a press emerged to express opinion and discuss problems. As in the other areas of Jewish life, the papers were written in French for the most part, and they were devoted to dealing with issues of acculturation.   Moderate religious reform was advocated by the paper *Archives Israélites* (founded in 1840), edited and published by Samuel Cahen, former teacher and translator of the Bible into French. A more conservative viewpoint, upholding orthodox tradition, was taken by the *L'Univers Israélite*, edited by Simon Bloch.[24]   In Alsace, *Lien d'Israel* and *Vérité* were very popular. Jewish acculturation was reflected in their new institutions and sometimes in their religious practices.

Clearly, by the 1840s Jews had achieved prominence and entry into the French economic and political life. Then in 1848, the French Revolution appeared as a threat, even though it emphasized the aspirations of the earlier upheaval of 1789, for Jews felt more secure in periods of order and stability. The Second Republic appointed the first Jewish ministers, a striking result of the general improvement of Jewish circumstances since 1789. These notable figures were Michel Goudchaux, Minister of Finance, and Adolph Crémieux, Minister of Justice,[25] who brought Jews a high level of visibility.

Although the Jews' position in France had improved, underlying antagonisms and long-held stereotypes remained as strong as ever in 1848. The new provisional government emphatically restated the tradition of human rights: freedoms of religion, press, and association. Immediately, the revolutionary enthusiasm and new freedom of the press led to a sudden efflorescence of newspapers, most of which were poorly financed and of little influence.

It was in such an atmosphere of political liberty that political antisemitism appeared as the weapon of the left, of socialism. The socialist papers, shrill and democratic in tone, were often short-lived in duration. A long established socialist antipathy toward Jews as the representatives of finance capitalism, and the quest for votes, led the left wing editors to use antisemitic language to convert their readers. The most tempting targets were, of course, Jewish bankers, the most notable of whom were the Rothschilds; but they also attacked the wealthy entrepreneurs, the railroads, and the new industries.[26] Much of the phraseology used was veiled: words such as "aliens" or phrases of the New Testament which were applicable to Jews. For instance, the *Voix des Clubs* declared that the "capitalists most of whom are not even French, lean heavily upon French property owners and workers."[27] The theme of the Jew as the alien was a reflection of xenophobia that was to persist as a strong tradition throughout the nineteenth and twentieth centuries. As early as the 1830s there was a continuous migration from Eastern Europe to France. From 1815 to the 1880s the immigration consisted largely of German Jews, with some Polish migrants. Later, after 1870, the largest number came from Eastern European shtetls. In any case, the immigrant Jew was far more religious than his French counterpart, and certainly was "foreign" in his behavior. The image of the Jew as being an alien and, therefore, different, was reinforced by this influx.

Another highly visible target were the Jewish ministers. One paper actually directed its opposition to the Republic by castigating Adolph Crémieux, the Minister of Justice, saying:

> A Jew has slipped into the heart of government,
> into a post that by necessity should be held by a

man known for his delicacy of soul, and by his political constancy, and this Jew (Cremieux) brings to
his high mission narrow views and a lack of morality. . . . Justice is the religion of France, we do not
wish its altars profaned by Jews; it is necessary that
they be chased from them.[28]

Antisemitism even played a minor role in the Bonapartist propaganda which sought working class support. Their few papers attacked the
wealthy with complete abandon: "The people are still under the yoke of
the aristocracy of money whose maneuvers precipitated the downfall of
Napoleon," adding that no one could acquire real wealth in twenty years,
except through dishonesty.[29] The temptation to attack Jews proved too politically advantageous to resist, and these papers too, used the words "foreigner" and Jew interchangeably. The *Napoleonien* complained that the "usurers and Jews are responsible for our hardships and miseries." Though antisemitism was a factor in the ephemeral working class Bonapartist press,
such language was not used by the government of Napoleon III during
the Second Empire.[30] Antisemitism as a policy was abandoned. The Bonapartist papers, imitative of socialist rhetoric, were short lived and insignificant.

More significant and enduring in influence, however, were the
theories of Fourier and Alphonse Toussenel upon the development of French
antisemitism. Fourier was both irritated and even angered by the success
of a rival socialist group, the Saint-Simonians. The fact that a very large
percentage of its members were Jewish was especially irksome to Fourier.
These men had begun to garner fame and power by their activity in railroad building and in the reorganization of French industry. The best
known of these figures were the Pereire Brothers, Rodrigues, Léon Halevy,
and Baron Gustave d'Eichthal. For Fourier, Jews were potent rivals, as well
as the symbols of commerce.

Thus Fourier claimed that "Jews by virtue of their dedication to trade
are the spies of all nations and frequently are informers and hangmen. . . ."[31]
He bitterly opposed Jewish emancipation, for he was convinced that Judaism bred (as a result of its religious doctrines) deceit, and encouraged usury
and non-productive work. In Fourier's judgment, the only way the Jew
could become acceptable to French society, was to become totally assimilated in both a material and a spiritual manner. He must cease being Jewish.[32]

The most influential writer of the period was Alphonse Toussenel. He
claimed that his most significant mentor was Fourier, but he echoed ideas

expressed by his contemporary, Louis Veuillot,[33] with whom he had work-ed when he had been employed by the ultramontane newspaper *La Paix*. In his book, *Les juifs rois de l'époque, Histoire de la féodalité financière*, he crea-ted the common stereotypes later exhumed by Drumont that Jews were usurious, clannish, deceitful, intolerant, and wealthy. He further enun-ciated ideas which were prevalent in ultramontane circles, for obviously he and Veuillot exerted influence upon each other. He, too, considered Protestants as corrupt as Jews, because both read the Old Testament which was based on tales of adultery, incest, rape, and murder. He also pointed out that Protestants were "merchants and birds of prey," like Jews.[34] A contemporary assessment of Toussenel in the 1850s and 1860s characterized him as "patient, of good humor, and of modest deportment and on only one issue did he lose his serenity." All the terrible problems of France were equated by him with 2 December, which halted the spread of Fourierist ideas. He further claimed ". . . The movement which the em-peror leads which is so socially evil and which will become a chronic condi-tion in France, is tyrannical industrialism or Jewish capitalism. . . . The moral depression into which France has descended is the responsibility of the em-pire and the Jews."[35] In private conversation Toussenel reiterated the per-sistent stereotype of the Jew as the foreigner, incapable of being assimi-lated. He further complained that France and French culture were being over-run by Germans, referring to the immigrant Jews Offenbach and Meyerbeer.[36]

These sentiments were also echoed in the works of Proudhon and his followers, some of whom were highly antagonistic to finance capitalism.[37] Proudhon was an enemy of the Roman Catholic Church, and was an espe-cially avowed foe of the Saint-Simonians. Jews were also associated with the leading banking institutions, and were frequently, as in the case of the Pereires, leading exponents of economic growth and modernity. These were the two movements that Proudhon detested. By identifying Jews with capitalism, they became his prime targets. Rothschild and Jews were the masters of finance and thus the enemies of the small entrepreneurs and artisans, those people Proudhon supported.[38]

The socialist animus that characterized Jews as the representatives of finance capitalism, and reflected in the articles of the left in the press of 1848, was also expressed in the campaign speeches of such men as Pierre Leroux. Leroux's antisemitism was less strident and more subtle, but he, too, was willing to attack the Jewish presence in France.[39]

After June Days (1848) and the Coup d'Etat of December (1851) the socialist movement was driven underground by government repression;

its press was muzzled, its constituency was sapped by prosperity. Socialist organizations were hounded by authorities, and their political influences were stifled.[40] Although socialism was driven into oblivion during the Empire, other forces emerged which supplied fuel to socialist antisemitism after 1870.

Napoleon III supported some of the ideological principles of Saint-Simon in economic affairs. He believed that the role of government was to actively promote economic and commercial expansion as well as social improvement while preserving and stimulating private enterprise. Hence, encouragement was granted to bankers and businessmen willing to undertake expansion and bold economic innovation. Many of these entrepreneurs were Jewish, men such as the Pereire brothers, Benoît Fould, and Mirès. Indeed, Achille Fould had become Minister of Finance from October 1849 to January 1852 when he assumed office as Minister of State and became a participant in the (Conseil privé) cabinet of the Emperor. The Péreires founded the Crédit Mobilier, a new banking institution which solicited public subscriptions as sources of investment for the expansion of industry and railroads.[41] Consequently, when scandals occurred in these innovative and sometimes overextended enterprises, Jews were involved and blamed. More ammunition was thus funnelled into Socialist stereotypes of Jews. The *Affaires* which involved Mirès and the Crédit Mobilier were never the magnitude of the Union Generale, yet they were sensational, as they publicized the irregular practices, bad judgements, and dubious actions of their participants. The 1860s reinforced prevalent socialist animosities which were later revived during the Third Republic.[42] However, far more persistent and destructive antisemitic activity pervaded Alsace Lorraine during and after the Revolution of 1848. Sometimes the disturbances in the provinces were considered a part of the general provincial jacquerie and urban insurrection characteristic of the revolution. Some historians have duly noted that Alsatians were motivated by the same intense social and economic distress and the political antagonisms that it fomented. They also claimed that the resultant antisemitic outbreaks derived primarily from the hardships caused by the usurious practices associated with Jews.[43] However, closer examination indicates that antisemitism was much deeper rooted and enduring than a mere response to economic malaise.

As already noted, many Jews provided the banking services, in addition to brokerage in grain and cattle, because historically they had been denied occupational privileges in agriculture or the crafts (except goldsmithing). They had been excluded also from most commercial enterprises except peddling rags and second hand goods. Hence, though the revolution of 1789 brought them into the economic mainstream, a very high percentage still were poor and disadvantaged.[44] To add to their difficulties, Jews in Alsace were slower to assimilate, and many in 1848 still spoke Yiddish and were ethnically loyal to Ashkenazic customs and practices. Larger numbers of Jews remained clustered in their encapsulated communities, maintaining their traditional Yeshivas and religious observances. Moreover, traditional Catholic attitudes perpetuated contempt and disdain. The church regarded Judaism as a morally inferior religion, chiefly significant as a forerunner of Christianity. Furthermore, socially and intellectually, Jews were also considered inferior because they had not fully assimilated.[45] The Archbishop of Strasbourg, Msgr. Raess, remained obdurately opposed to the aspirations of the revolution and in January 1858 he described Catholic Alsace as a province firmly committed to legitimacy and as supportive of authority as it had been in 1848 and 1849.[46] As for Jews, his attitude firmly ultramontane, was disdainful of religious toleration.

The outbreaks in Alsace seemed very similar to those in the rest of France: its peasants were badly affected by the economic recession and its industries had also been affected by the disruptions of revolution. However, analysis of the widespread disorders throughout France revealed differences between Alsace and other areas.

When the news of the Revolution of 1848 reached the provinces, especially in the poorer mountainous regions of Basses-Alpes, Var, Drôme, Isere, Hautes-Alpes, many peasants expressed their frustration by attacking local landlords or the foresters, burning homes, uprooting grape arbors, killing livestock, and in general by a wanton, aimless vandalism. The peasants were desirous of retrieving the old rights to the use of the forests, which either were leased to the local proprietors or were managed by a government forester, and they thought the Revolution would restore their former privileges.[47]

In some regions, protest erupted against taxes. The republic had imposed a forty-five centime tax which brought great hardship to the small or marginal peasant proprietor. Resistance to the payment of taxes was very widespread and bitter, especially in the poor agricultural regions of France.[48] Riots and demonstrations to protest the tax were common, as local tax collectors were threatened physically, and communal offices were set on fire to destroy records.[49] Although crop failure and low prices caused rural depression, conditions were further aggravated by industrial slowdown. The revolution itself exacerbated these conditions, and the widespread restlessness necessitated the stationing of troops to preserve order.[50] In Limoges the unemployed, furious over the outcome of the elections, broke into the City Hall and occupied it for several days.[51] In Lyons and surrounding sections working people, sometimes aided by soldiers, entered factories and destroyed machines.[52] Other areas also reported extensive damage to machinery, pillage, and arson, particularly to the railroads. These Luddite-type manifestations were punctuated by frequent strikes, some of which were violent.[53] The obsession of the workers with jobs and pay led to a nasty reaction to foreign workers in France. Further, politicization of these grievances provided the network for the development of both republican and socialist organized movements.[54]

In the department of the Nord, Belgian unskilled laborers were the target, but they were allowed to stay.[55] In Lyons and Bourges, Italian migrants became the handy scapegoats.[56] Protest was marked by action against specific economic targets which represented oppression. This sporadic violent behavior reflected dissatisfaction with economic and social conditions.

The sporadic violence in Alsace seemed to resemble the jacquerie type uprising throughout the rest of France. Although the Alsatian riots appeared to be directed against social and economic targets of oppression and hardship,[57] there were significant differences. Firstly, the depression also hit the developing textile industry in Alsatian cities, but unlike other urban areas there was minimal unrest in the cities. Most of the violence occurred in the countryside or in the smaller communes in which Jewish communities were largely concentrated. There was no question that anger was being expressed by the peasants at the burden imposed by their debts to Jewish moneylenders.[58] What, however, distinguished the violence in Alsace-Lorraine from the rest of the country was that aggressive mob behavior was not directed against the usurer or the wealthy peasant alone, or even specific political targets, but against *all Jews* rich, poor, oppressor and oppressed. Report after report described demonstrations and personal attacks against Jews.[59]

One official, Schongreen from Colmar, noted that: "In Oberdorf the mobs attacked the Jews, although they (the Jews) were almost all indigent. Everywhere the mobs started by attacking the synagogues, although the synagogues engage in neither trade nor usury."[60] In many communes it was necessary to seek the aid of the national guard or troops to maintain any semblance of order.[61] In other villages, Jews abandoned their homes and businesses and fled fearing for their lives.[62] A contemporary account of the disorders stated:

> In Alsace, the peasant is the irreconcilable enemy of the Jew and he (the peasant) feels that Jewish property has been gained through usury. At the appropriate moment he thus attacks all Israelites without discriminating between the usurers and those who are honest. . . . These explosions are warranted by anger and hate against the usurer who is often Jewish. However, prejudice against Jews is so strong that the mobs attack all Jews. In the Commune of Hegenheim where there were no usurers at all, the mobs pillaged the poorest homes, and they destroyed the house of a widow who regularly contributed a third of her income to the poor without regard to their religion.[63]

Even in the town of Durmenach, which seemed to have established good interfaith relations by the election of a Jewish mayor, the same pattern of irrational disturbances took place. There, mobs attacked twenty-five Jewish members of the National Guard. Lynching was averted only by the concerted and cooperative efforts of the local priest and rabbi.[64] Jews did not always remain passive in the face of these provocations. In the village of Hegenheim, they had become self confident enough to organize, and they had defended themselves so vigorously against their enemies "that the miserable wretches were forced to retire."[65] This highly visible and virulent anti-semitism did not cease with the end of the revolution. The rest of the country returned to economic development and its accompanying prosperity, and government repression ended deep-seated social protest and its accompanying violence. Only in Alsace did minor eruptions of violence continue throughout the Second Empire: a harsh reminder both to the authorities and the Jewish consistories of the threats of antisemitism that embraced Alsace.[66] Another distinguishing factor of the disorders in the Alsatian provinces was the widespread support and sympathy for the demonstrators. In the rest of France, the established authorities and the middle classes were horrified by the continual social upheavals and the property damage which often ensued. It was reflected in support of order and the extensive victories of conservative deputies and officials in the general elections. Although Alsace was conservative and generally its middle classes were alarmed by the June Days, they were quite willing to permit the depredations, pillaging, and enormous property damage of the Jews. [67]

The central government, devoted to revolutionary principles and to the concept of the sanctity of private property, was both irritated and disturbed by these violent outbreaks. The administration, therefore, sent strongly worded instructions demanding that order must be maintained, property rights must be preserved, and respect for civil rights of all citizens must be protected. Only the assurance of swift, firm justice, unhesitatingly enforced, could reestablish peace and security. To that end, therefore, the Paris administration sent instructions that every effort be directed to the enforcement of law. The directives stated, "The provisional government feels that these riots compromise the Republic and the Revolution. . . . We are counting on your vigilance and firmness to see that the perpetrators of these disturbances are fully prosecuted."[68] Another official reminded the local authorities that the Israelites of the departments of the East must cease being the victims of local aggressions because since the February Revolution (1848) Jews and their property must be respected exactly the same as all members of the French family.[69] Circulars were distributed to the mayors of the communes stating unequivocally that all Frenchmen were equal and all enjoyed liberty of worship. Further, they (the mayors) must inform their constituents "that if Israelites' homes or any others were pillaged or devastated, the commune *must sooner or later pay damages and indemnify the owners.*"[70]

Yet, despite all these remonstrances and the numerous arrests which followed, both the procureurs and the Jews were unable to obtain enforcement of order, or punishment for wrong-doers. Groups of demonstrators at the prisons often intimidated officials to release prisoners,[71] and during trials juries frequently acquitted the defendants despite incriminating evidence.[72] The judges frequently meted out lenient sentences for the few that were convicted. The Jewish consistories, disturbed at the miscarriage of justice, requested that the minister of religion and the minister of justice enact stronger measures to protect their co-religionists in Alsace-Lorraine. They further suggested that the prosecutions of rioters required a change in venue, in order to ensure an unbiased jury and a firmer administration of justice.[73] The procureurs responded to the pleas of the Jews and the government orders by agreeing with the need for firmness, but they complained that it was impossible to enforce. "To push prosecution too hard," the district attorney noted, "would be impolitic and dangerous; it would wound the sensibilities of the provinces and would provoke even more demonstrations."[74] In general, local officials tended to interpret government directives in a manner sympathetic to local public opinion, behavior which these good bureaucrats continued throughout the Second Empire.

Official attitudes toward antisemitism did not change, even though the edicts of the republic were enforced only sometimes at the local level. Lawsuits were begun to obtain compensation for the loss of Jewish homes and furniture, and for the rebuilding of synagogues in the communes of Durmenach, Oberdorff and Hegenheim. These were continued during the Second Empire. In one case, that of Hegenheim, the government lawyers cited the Law of Vendemaire as the precedent for making the town responsible for payment of damages. Adolph Crémieux argued the Jewish cause eloquently for over seven hours. It was not enough, as the Jews lost their case, and they, the plaintiffs, were ordered to pay the court expenses. The court's judgement was based on demography; the population of Hegenheim consisted of 200 families (105 of which were Jewish). The government appealed and the decision was eventually reversed.[75] On the other hand, the majority of cases won reparations from the courts. In most cases, the awards were double the actual amount of the damages, because the judges decreed that the victims should be compensated for their suffering and inconvenience.[76]

Unfortunately, anti-Jewish outbursts characterized by sporadic violence did not end in Alsace during the Second Empire. Religious differences were more strident in that province and open antagonisms between Catholics and Protestants often resulted in demonstrations.[77] The surface manifestations of antisemitism were readily stimulated by economic and religious crisis. Depression was widespread throughout France in 1857, and Alsace was no exception. Economic distress fueled hostilities. There were several minor incidents: hooting, demonstrations, open clashes, but there were no widespread pogrom-type looting and general mayhem that had been prevalent in 1848. Moreover, officials reacted quickly to prevent such behavior by stationing police, and generally assuming a law and order posture. Nevertheless, they continued to avoid prosecution of the offenders, preferring to placate the populace and command good will for the government.[78] They wished order and stability, and used firmness and conciliation as their means of dealing with the situation. Furthermore, the procureurs' reluctance to push punishment for the Alsatian ruffians rested upon their own prejudices. They too, often believed that it was the problem of Jewish usurers and their high interest charges that aroused bitterness among the Catholic population. As one procureur wrote:

> . . . A considerable part of the Alsatian Jews seem
> to remain apart from the rest of our population.

Maintaining the trade of their origin, without roots in our country, they have refused to engage in business or agriculture, and instead exploit through the most hostile trade the poorest inhabitants of our country-side. . . . Creditors of considerable wealth, they hold the country under their domination and lead our peasantry into a state of misery and demoralization comparable only to the Irish peasants. As long as this irritation exists, it will ferment with-out cessation, violence, pillage, and devastation.[79]

The image of the grasping usurer became a fixed stereotype within the Alsatian community. The truth was that Jewish creditors provided an important and necessary financial service for the beleaguered peasants; Jews provided funds for the day-to-day operations of the peasant and were the middlemen in brokering crops and cattle. Payments for these services seemed to be in the range of eight to ten percent interest rates, not excessive at that time. Moreover, there were very few rich Jews in Alsace; the exception perhaps, was the Ratisbonne family.[80] Nevertheless, the imputation of Jewish wrongdoing remained a potent enduring calumny that poisoned civility and worsened the already strained religious hostilities. Thus, ultramontane denunciations of religious differences were reinforced by negative economic prejudices and intensified both the apprehensions and the suspicions of rival groups.

The Jewish community had not forgotten 1848 (only nine years before) and they were apprehensive, nervous, and fearful. Any disturbance, no matter how minor, aroused both terror and suspicion. The consistories desired stiffer penalties and more overt demonstration of police power. Even after 1857 when prosperity returned, there were occasional incidents involving youths throwing stones and fighting over religious differences.[81] Since the government's major goal was the maintenance of peace and stability, officials pursued aims of reconciliation between the diverse groups in Alsace-Lorraine. Priests who preached inflammatory antisemitic or anti-Protestant sermons in areas where Catholics were the minority were transferred from their pulpits, and attempts were made to regulate the flow of antisemitic writings. Efforts were made to reduce the tensions caused by "Jewish usury."[82] Alsatian antisemitism reinforced socialist rhetoric, but that movement was effectively repressed during the Second Empire.

Instead, antisemitism emerged as a powerful current in the thought and nationalist passion of the extreme right: the ultramontanes and their allies. These were groups who resented the loss of the special privileges which they had possessed before the French Revolution. Strengthening these animosities, created by rapid change, was the traditional antisemitism which was firmly embedded in the religious teachings of the Roman Catholic Church. The Church was strongly opposed to the concept of religious freedom.[83] Religion and politics had never been separated in France, and antisemitism subsequently became embroiled in the emerging conflicts between church and state. The church itself was divided on questions of modernity, freedom, and tolerance, and in the controversies caused by the revolution of 1848, reluctantly supported Louis Napoleon and the Second Empire.[84] This alliance was established after June Days as Louis Napoleon wooed varied political constituencies in French society in his quest for election to the French presidency. He had already used the Napoleonic Legend and his book, *Extinction of Pauperism*, to gain working class and peasant sympathy. He was, however, appalled by the disorder and radicalism of June Days, and saw the Church as the bulwark of order and stability. Hence he promised to uphold the interests of the Church. In addition, if he was to achieve victory, he would have to enlist the aid of the nation's "notables," the important men in the various French communities. June Days had frightened conservatives, and they, in turn, responded to Louis Napoleon because they felt he could restore order. By capitalizing upon his reputation for authority he recruited De Broglie, Barrot, Carlier, Emile Thomas, Thiers, all of whom sought stability and restoration. These men had abandoned hope for their Legitimist and Orleanist candidates' success, and they were suspicious of Cavaignac republicanism. Louis Napoleon seemed the best of a "bad bargain." They formed a party of Order and reluctantly joined the Bonapartist campaign. They made a temporary political alliance because they preferred monarchy and expected Louis Napoleon to enhance the Church's influence.

Thus the tentative alliance also tended to the Church's interests. The ultramontanes assumed at that time that only the Bonapartes could protect the Church, family, and tradition against the excesses of the "red" revolutionaries. On the other hand, Louis Napoleon needed their support, however unenthusiastic, to assure his victory and his throne. Nevertheless it was, and remained, an alliance of convenience, proffered with little enthusiasm by either side. Louis Napoleon was a devout believer in at least some of the principles of 1789, while many of his conservative political allies were not. The ultramontanes wished the church to gain a larger control of education and more privileges in the established political order. Louis Napoleon desired the strengthening of the Church only as a bulwark against revolutionary excesses to assure stability, but he always insisted that the church remain subordinated to the needs of the secular state. Many conservatives wished the church to maintain a religious monopoly; while the Prince-President (later the Emperor) fervently accepted the principle of religious toleration and equality. Inevitably conflicts would surface in the debates over the proper relationship between Church and State. Unfortunately, Jewish issues often became embroiled in this struggle, and antisemitic polemics were inserted in the ultramontane press.

The French government supported the ideal of religious freedom, and actively encouraged and reinforced Jewish minority rights. This official attitude was reflected by a series of positive actions. All barriers to equal educational opportunity (based on merit) were removed. Prior to the Bonapartist regime, the policy, which was often demanded by the Church, had excluded Jewish students and professors from either attending or teaching in many schools. That practice, despite pressure from the Catholic clergy was disavowed. When a professional school in Toulouse passed regulations that required students to show a baptismal certificate for admittance, the Minister of Religion ordered the directors of the institution to abolish that regulation or admit Jewish students without certificates.[85] In the district of Maçon, school regulations which established Catholic religious instruction for all students was immediately negated by the Minister of Religion.[86] Government officials did not hesitate to appoint Jewish professors and scholars to important academic posts even over protest and pressure by the Catholic clergy.[87]

French foreign policy, likewise, reflected the overt protection of religious freedom, continuing the traditions of the Second Republic.[88] Napoleon III defended Roman Jews in 1849, and subsequently, in 1858, 1861, and 1864.[89] Other examples of such policies were attested to by the French efforts to protect Roumanian Jews in the Treaty of 1858 which reorganized the Roumanian Principalities of Moldavia and Wallachia.[90] Again in the 1860s, French insistence on Jewish rights were negotiated in the trade treaties with the Swiss government.[91]

In internal affairs, too, the authoritarian structure of the administration was sometimes used to prosecute vicious antisemitism. Such a case occurred in 1858 when a book entitled *Vrai et faux Catholiques* was seized by the police. The author, M. Martin, advocated the extermination of both

Jews and Protestants. He condemned religious toleration and insisted that the Church should extirpate both heretics and infidels. The Inquisition was hailed as a fine institution and the mass slaughter of Jews was highly praised. The court not only seized this book, but condemned the author to six months imprisonment and levied a fine of 2000 francs. The judges' harsh sentence was based on the arguments that Martin had exceeded the limits allowed by the law for the practice of free discussion. The judges noted that in this book, the author attacked religious freedom and undermined respect for the laws and the constitution of the French state.[92]

Censorship of the theater provided yet another arena through which antisemitic rhetoric was circumscribed. On 30 July 1850, dramatic censorship was established (the legislation was similar to that passed in the reign of Louis-Philippe). Authorization had to be obtained from the Minister of the Interior (for Paris), and from the prefects in the departments, before production of a play was permitted.[93] However, in the year 1853, the Minister of Interior shifted the duties of censorship for the Parisian theaters to the Minister of State of the Household of the Emperor. The Minister of State was Achille Fould (a prominent Jewish banker who had converted to Protestantism), who was most sympathetic to Jewish sensibilities. His supportive attitude was evidenced by his reaction to the comic opera, *Don Pedre*. A Jew was portrayed in this play in a defamatory stereotype, commonly accepted in the nineteenth century. A few days after the play opened in Paris, the newspaper *Archives Israélites* criticized French playwrights for their delineation of Jewish characters. Fould, stung by this comment, investigated the journal's complaints, and finding them justified, issued written instructions that all pejorative references be eradicated from scenes of the play. In 1854, before the opening performance of *The Jew of Venice* (a translation of *The Merchant of Venice*), Fould insisted that the characterization of Shylock be softened so as not to awaken religious animosities.[94] Another play by Victor Sejour, entitled *Richard III*, contained a reference: "Jews, the scum of humanity, shameful reprobates of mankind," which was immediately deleted by the censor.[95] Fould had created the precedent, which led the theatrical censors to treat the depiction of Jews in plays with great circumspection, subsequently forcing playwrights to eliminate unfavorable and distasteful portrayals. This practice continued throughout the Second Empire.

Thus Jews enjoyed what seemed full acceptance into French society. Emancipation and the encouragement of innovative entrepreneurship created new wealth, new opportunities and new occupations in which Jews excelled and achieved social and economic mobility. Nevertheless, the Jewish community, as well as individuals, felt threatened, and even marginal, while seeking approval and acceptance. When antisemitism, often just a by-product of ideological and political debates, sometimes surfaced during the Second Empire, wealthier Jews feared that the Jewish community as a whole would be held liable for the inadequacies and failures of their individual members. Therefore, they felt constrained to assist their co-religionists in achieving the educational and cultural levels of the French upper classes. What emerged was the proliferation of various communal charitable and educational institutions, dominated by Jewish economic elites which were secular rather than religious. These communal associations also provided a focus through which Jews in the Second Empire would respond (sometimes timorously) when they felt threatened; a new behavior when contrasted to their victimized attitudes of 1789.[96] Thus, in spite of a friendly government and their increased economic power, Jews felt threatened by individual incidents; but they had become capable of articulating their concerns. They were no longer willing to remain mute or passive in the face of threats to their well-being.

The first major challenge to which the Jews responded occurred in 1840. The death of a priest in the city of Damascus aroused the old charges of Jewish ritual murder among the populace. This led to widespread rioting and persecution of the Jews. Leaders of the French and British Jews (Sir Moses Montefiore, Adolph Crémieux, and Solomon Munk) went to Egypt and petitioned Mohamet Ali to stop the harassment of their co-religionists.[97] The event illustrated that Jews now had the means to act in the face of problems of their brethren; it also revealed the absence for the Jews of Western Europe of any organized groups which could cope with such situations as they arose throughout the world. It would take two more decades and a new crisis, that of Edgardo Mortara, to organize institutions to deal with such problems.[98] The Mortara Affair emerged as a crisis which was to become significant in not only the development of Jewish responses, but also as a divisive conflict between church and state. The issue will be explored in the next chapter.

1 c. f. John M. Merriman, *The Agony of the Republic*, (New Haven, London: Yale Univ. Press, 1978).

2 J. F. C. Harrison, *The Second Coming: Popular Millenarianism 1750-1850*, (New Brunswick, N.J.: Rutgers Univ. Press, 1979); Norman Cohn, *The Pursuit of the Millenium*, 2nd edition (New York: Harper and Row, 1961); François Lebrun, *Histoire des catholiques en France du XV siècle à nos jours*, (Toulouse: Privat, 1980), 291-368.

3 Thomas Kselman, *Miracles and Prophecies in Nineteenth Century France*, (New Brunswick, N.J.: Rutgers University Press,1983); Marcel Launay, "Le diocèse de Nantes, Monseigneur Jacquemet (1848-1869)," *L'Information Histoire*, 44 (1982): 208-18; c. f. Michael J. Phayer, *Sexual Liberation and Religion in Nineteenth Century Europe*, (London: Croom Held,1977), 113-4.

4 Robert F. Byrnes, *Antisemitism in Modern France*, (New York: Howard Fertig, 1969); Michael R. Marrus, *The Politics of Assimilation, a Study of the French Jewish Community at the Time of the Dreyfus Affair*, (Oxford: Clarendon Press, 1971); Pierre Pierrard, *Juifs et catholiques français*, (Paris: Fayard, 1970) does include some mention of the Second Empire; Jacob Katz, *From Prejudice to Destruction, Antisemitism, 1700-1933*, (Cambridge, Mass.: Harvard University Press, 1980), 107-44, has a fine chapter on the earlier manifestations of anti-semitism in France.

5 Zeldin, *France*, I, 1026; Paula Hyman, *From Dreyfus to Vichy, the Remaking of French Jewry*, (New York: Columbia University Press, 1979), 1-31.

6 Robert A. Kann, "Assimilation and Antisemitism in the German-French Orbit in the Nineteenth and Early Twentieth Centuries," *Leo Baeck Institute Yearbook*, 14 (1969): 92-115.

7 Stephen Sharot, *Judaism, A Sociology*, (New York: Holmes and Meier, 1976), 100.

8 I. Leveillant, "La génèse de l'antisémitisme sous la Troisième République," *Révue des Études juives*, 53 (1907): 66-89.

9 *Jewish Chronicle*, (London), 22 January 1858.

10 Jacob Katz, *Emancipation and Assimilation, Studies in Modern Jewish History*, (Farnborough, England: Greggs, 1972), 4-6.

11 c. f. Samuel Posener, "The Social Life of the Jewish Communities in France," *Jewish Social Studies*, 7 (1945): 229-30.

12 Cerf-Berr was one of the notable Alsatian figures urging more integration. c. f. Raphael Mahler, *A History of Modern Jewry 1780-1815*, (New York: Shocken, 1971); I. E. Ginsburger, "Les familles Lehman et Cerf Berr," *Revue des Études juives*, 49 (1910): 106-30.

13 Rosemary Ruether, *Faith and Fraticide*, (New York: Seabury Press, 1974).

14 Robert Holtman, *The Napoleonic Revolution*, (New York: Lippincott, 1967), 132-37; for a detailed study c.f. David Feuerwerker, *L'émancipation des juifs en France de l'Ancien Régime à la fin du Second Empire*, (Paris: Michel, 1976); Georges Lefebvre, *Napoleon from Tilst to Waterloo, 1807-1815*, (New York: Columbia Univ. Press, 1969), 186-97; Simon Schwarzfuchs, *Napoleon, the Jews and the Sanhedrin*, (London, Boston: Routledge and Kegan, 1979).

[15] Hugo Valentin, *Antisemitism: Historically and Critically Examined*, (New York: Viking Press, 1936), 50.

[16] Byrnes, *Antisemitism in Modern France*, Léon Poliakov, *History of Antisemitism III, From Voltaire to Wagner*, (New York: Vanguard Press, 1976); Philippe Bourdrel, *Histoire des juifs de France*, (Paris: A. Michel, 1974); I. Elbogen, *A Century of Jewish Life*, (Phila.: Jewish Publication Society, 1960); Feuerwerker, *L'emancipation des juifs*; Schwarzfuchs, *Les juifs de France*.

[17] David Cohen, "L'image du juif dans la société française en 1843, d'après les rapports de préfets," *Revue d'Histoire économique et sociale*, 55 (1977): 88-91; c. f. Jacob Katz, *Out of the Ghetto: The Social Background of Jewish Emancipation 1770-1870*, (Cambridge, Mass., Harvard Univ. Press, 1973).

[18] Schwarzfuchs, *Les juifs de France*, 245-47; A. F. Hewit, "Ratisbonne, Alphonse, Conversion from Judaism," *Catholic World*, 39 (1884): 613-26.

[19] Jacob Katz, "Religion as a Uniting and Dividing Force," in Jacob Katz, ed. *The Role of Religion in Modern Jewish History*, (Cambridge, Mass: Harvard University Press, 1973), 6-9; Natalie Isser and Lita L. Schwartz, *History of Conversion and Contemporary Cults*, (New York: Peter Lang, 1988), 3-10.

[20] David Cohen, *La promotion des juifs en France à l'époque du Second Empire 1852-1870*, (Université de Provence, 1982), II, 719-20; Katz, *Emancipation and Assimilation*, 195.

[21] *Jewish Chronicle*, (London); *Archives Israélites*; *L'Univers Israélite* had innumerable articles describing and criticizing missionary activities; c. f. Isser and Schwartz, *History of Conversion . . .*, chapters. II, III.

[22] Barrie M. Ratcliffe, "Crisis and Identity: Gustave d'Eichthal and Judaism in the Emancipation Period," *Jewish Social Studies*, 37 (1975): 122-40.

[23] Zosa Szajkowski, *Jewish Education in France, 1789-1939*, (New York: Columbia University Press, 1980), 11-30.

[24] Schwarzfuchs, *Les juifs de France*, 251.

[25] For more about these men c. f. Samuel Posener, *Adolph Crémieux*, (Phila. Publication Society, 1940); Raymond Lazard, *Michel Goudchaux, 1797-1862, son oeuvre et vie politique*, (Paris: Alcan, 1907).

[26] For more about these new bankers and entrepreneurs, see Chapter V.

[27] *La Voix des Clubs*, 22 March 1848.

[28] *Père Duchêne*, 9 May 1848.

[29] *L'Organisation du Travail*, 8, 9, 11, 14, 15 June 1848.

[30] Robert Pimienta, *La propagande bonapartiste en 1848*, (Paris, 1911), 160-62.

[31] Charles Silberner, "Charles Fourier on the Jewish Question," *Jewish Social Studies*, 8 (1946): 246-48.

[32] Ibid.; Robert Byrnes, 118-120.

[33] Zosa Szajkowsi, "The Jewish Saint-Simonians and Socialist Antisemitism in France, *Jewish Social Studies*, 9 (1947): 47.

24

34 Ibid.; Georges Weill, "Les Saint-Simonians sous Napoléon III," *Revue des Études Napoleoniennes*, I (1912): 391-406.

35 Juliette Adam, *Mes premières armes*, (Paris, 1894), 138-39.

36 Ibid.

37 Szajkowski, "Jewish Saint-Simonians," 60-63; Byrnes, 115; 119-125; c. f. Silberner, "Charles Fourier on the Jewish Question," 245-59.

38 Szajkowski , "Jewish Saint-Simonians," 60-63; Simon Schama, *Two Rothschilds and the Land of Israel*, (New York: Alfred A, Knopf, 1978), 44-46

39 Edmund Silberner, "Pierre Leroux's Ideas on the Jewish People," *Jewish Social Studies*, 12 (1950): 383-84.

40 c. f. Merriman, *The Agony of the Republic*.

41 Bourd, 179-82; Paul Emden, *Money Powers of Europe*, (New York: Appleton-Century, 1938), 139-60; c. f. Louis Girard, *La politique des travaux publics du Second Empire*, (Paris: Colin, 1952).

42 For further discussion of these Affaires see Chap. V.

43 Edward Stadtler, "Die Judenkrawalle von 1848 im Elsäss," *Elsässiche Monatsschrift fur Geschichte und Volkskunde*, 2 (1911): 673-86; G. Cahen, " Les juifs et la vie économique des campagnes (1648-1870)," *Revue d'Alsace*, 97 (1958): 141-46.

44 Zosa Szajkowski, *Poverty and Social Welfare Among French Jews 1800-1850*, (New York: 1954).; Nathan Netter, *Vingt siècles d'histoire d'une communauté juive*, (Paris: Libraire Lipschutz, 1938).

45 Jacob Katz, "Religion as a Uniting and Dividing Force," in Katz (ed.) *Role of Religion*, 7; Eugene Weber, *Peasants into Frenchmen: The Modernization of Rural France 1870-1914*. Stanford, Ca.: Stanford University Press, 1976), 39.

46 Fernand L'Huillier, "L'attitude politique de Mgr. Raess entre 1859 et 1879," *Études Alsaciennes*: Société savante d'Alsace et des regions de l'Est, 1947; 245-61.

47 Procureur Reports, Aix, 1, 2, 3, 4, 8, 11 March; 17, 19, 21, April; 4, 6, 7, 11, 18, 19 June 1848, Archives Nationales, MSS, Paris, BB30, 358 (hereafter referred to as AN, carton no.); Police Reports, Lambesc, 3 March 1848, Marseilles, Archives Departementales, MSS, M6 (hereafter referred to as AD); Procureur Reports, Grenoble, 19, 21 March 1848, AN, BB30, 360; Procureur Report, Toulouse, 23 March, AN, BB30, 365; Albert Soboul, "La question paysanne en 1848," *Pensée*, 18-19 (1948): 55-66, 19-37; Maurice Agulhon, *The Republican Experiment 1848-1852*, (Cambridge, London: Cambridge Univ. Press, 1983): 44-48.

48 Ibid; Peter Amann, "Changing of Outlines of 1848," *American Historical Review* , 68 (July 1963): 948-49.

49 Procureur Reports, Aix, 17, 18 , 19 June 1848, AN, BB30, 358; Procureur Reports, Lons-Le-Saunier, 2, 7, June 1848, BB 30, 359; Procureur Reports, Amiens, 26 May; 31 October 1848, BB30, 360; Procureur Reports, Dijon, 19 March 1848; 16, 17 June 1848, AN BB30, 361; Remi Gossez, "La résistance à l'impôt les quarante centimes," *Études, Société d'histoire de la*

Revolution de 1848, (Paris,1953), 77.

[50] Police Reports, Lyons, 3, 26, 31 March 1848, AD, M6.

[51] Cours d'Assises de Vienne, Affaire de Limoges, 30 April 1848, AN, BB30, 361.

[52] Police Reports, 3, 30 March; 6 April 1848, AD, M6; Procureur Reports, St. Etienne, 30 March 1848; Roanne, 8, 10 March; Lyons, 17, 21 April; 19 May; 6 June 1848, AN, BB30, 361.

[53] Procureur Reports, Riom, 29, 30 June 1848, An BB30, 365; Procureur Reports, Toulouse, 14 April; 17, 25 March; 9 May; 20 June 1848, AN, BB30, 359

[54] c. f. Merriman, *The Agony of the Republic.*

[55] Lord Normanby, *Memoirs of a Year of Revolution*, (Paris, 1848), I, 305.

[56] Procureur Report, Bourges, 29 March 1848.

[57] Edouard Stadtler, "Die Judenkrawalle von 1848 in Elsässe," *Elsässiche Monatsschrift fur Geschichte und Volkskunde*, 2 (1911): 673-86; Moses Ginsburger, "Les Troubles contre des juifs d'Alsace en 1848," *Revue des Études juives*, 64 (1912): 209-17.

[58] Procureur Reports, Colmar, 4 March; 8, 20, 21 April; 3, 4, 7, 8, May; 7 September; 21 December 1848, AN BB 30, 360.

[59] Procureur Reports, Colmar, 28, 29 February; 4 March; 8, 20, 21, April; 3, 4, 6, 12 May; 12 July; 17 October; 21 December 1848, AN, BB30, 360.

[60] Procureur Reports, Colmar, 4 March; 8, 20, 21 April; 3, 4, 7, 8, May; 7 September; 21 December 1848, AN, BB30, 360.

[61] Procureur Reports, Colmar, 28, 29 February; 4 March; 8, 20, 21 April; 3, 4, 6, 12 May; 12 July; 17 October; 21 December 1848, AN, BB30, 360.

[62] Mario Rossi, "Emancipation of the Jews of Italy," in A. Duker and Ben Horin (eds.) *Emancipation and Counter-Emancipation*, (New York: Ktav, 1974), 16.

[63] Consistory of Colmar to the Minister of Justice, 26 May 1848, AN, F 19, 11031.

[64] Procureur Reports, Colmar, 4 March; 8, 20, 21 April; 26 May 1848, AN, BB30, 360.

[65] Ibid.

[66] Rossi, *Emancipation and Counter-Emancipation*, 169

[67] Phyllis Cohen Albert, *The Modernization of French Jewry: Consistory and Community in the Nineteenth Century*, (Hanover, New Hampshire: Brandeis Univ. Press, 1977): 159-60; N. M. Kahan-Rabecq, "Comment le departement de Haut-Rhin devint Bonapartiste," *Révolution de 1848*, 32 (1936): 134-40; c. f. Paul Müller, "Le Bas Rhin de 1848 à 1852," *Révolution de 1848*, 6 (1910): 353-66.

[68] Procureur Report, Colmar, 2 March 1848, AN, BB30, 360.

[69] Ibid., 26 May 1848.

[70] Ibid., Circular to Mayors. The italicized words were also italicized in the Circular.

[71] Procureur Report, Colmar, 2 March 1848, BB30, 360.

[72] Ibid., Central Israelite Consistory to Minister of Religion, 29 February; 4 July 1848; AN, F 19, 11031.

[73] Ibid., Rabbi of Hegenheim, 19 May 1848, An, F 19, 11031; Moses E. Ginsburger, "Les

troubles contre les juifs d'Alsace en 1848," *Revue des Études juives*, 64 (1912): 110-12.

74 Procureur Report Colmar, 29 May 1848, AN, BB30, 360.

75 *Jewish Chronicle*, (London), 7 March 1851; *L'Industriel Alsacien*, 20 April 1851 cited in *Jewish Chronicle*, (London), 6, 23 April 1851.

76 Ibid.; *Archives Israélites*, September 1859.

77 Natalie Isser, "Proselytization and Protestants during the Second Empire," *Journal of Church and State*, 30 (Winter 1988): 51-70.

78 Albert, 160.; Jean Maurain, *Politique ecclésiastique du Second Empire*, (Paris: Alcan, 1930), 386-87.

79 Procureur Report, March 1853, AN, BB30, 376.

80 David Cohen, *La Promotion des juifs en France à l'époque du Empire 1852-1870*, (Doctoral Thesis, Université de Provence, 1982), II, 674-95.

81 *Archives Israélites*, January 1860.

82 Ibid.

83 Gene Benardini, "The Origins and Development of Racial Antisemitism in Fascist Italy," *Journal of Modern History*, 49 (1977): 432; Arnold Ages, *The Diaspora Dimension*, (Hague: Nijhoff, 1973), 6-10; Léon Poliakov, "Antisemitism and Christian Teaching," *Midstream*, 13 (1966): 13-18; Jules Isaac, *The Teaching of Contempt*, (New York: Rinehart & Winston, 1964), 21-35.

84 Austin Gough, *Paris and Rome*, (Oxford: Clarendon Press, 1986): 51-80.

85 *Archives Israélites*, December 1854.

86 Ibid.

87 Ibid., March 1856. Professor A. Frank was such a case.

88 Natalie Isser, "The Revolution of 1848 and Human Rights," J. Sweet, ed., *Proceedings of Western Society for French History*, 12 (1985): 129-39.

89 Adrien Dansette, *Religious History of Modern France*, (New York: Herder & Herder, 1961), 263.

90 Hübner to Buol, Paris, 15 August 1858, MSS, Vienna. Haus-Hof-and Staatsarchiv, IX, 57.

91 Natalie Isser, "Diplomatic Intervention and Human Rights, the Swiss Question." Paper presented at Ohio Valley History Conference, 1986.

92 *Jewish Chronicle*, (London), 29 January 1858; *Archives Israélites*, February 1858.

93 Alveric Cahuet, *La liberté de théâtre en France*, (Paris: Dujarric, 1902), 218-19; Circulaire, *La censure dramatique*, (Paris, 1892), 82-84.

94 Victor Hallays-Dabot, *La censure dramatique et le théâtre*, (Paris, 1871), 92-96.

95 Charles E. O'Neill, "Theatrical Censorship in France," *Harvard Library Bulletin*, 26 (1978): 440-41.

96 Katz, *Emanicipation and Assimilation*, 195; Albert, 158-166.

97 Simon Schwarzfuchs, *Les juifs de France*, (Paris: Albin Michel, 1945), 251.

98 Ibid., 261-62.

Chapter II

The Mortara Affair

One of the most strident and divisive controversies to dominate both the political debate and the press of the Second Empire was the Mortara Affair, centered around events in 1858 that occurred in Bologna, in the Papal States. On the evening of 23 June 1858, Marmalo and Marianna Mortara were awakened by the entry of several men, who demanded that their child, Edgardo (at that moment six years, ten months of age), be remanded to the custody of the state by order of the Chief Inquisitor, Father Feletti of Bologna. Marmalo Mortara protested, and his wife, Marianna, beside herself, screamed in anguish; the police, moved by the parents' pleading, gave them a stay of twenty-four hours. Relatives and friends in the Ghetto, informed of the circumstances by an older Mortara son, raised funds to ransom the small Edgardo. However, such efforts would prove to be of no avail. At the same moment Marmalo Mortara and his brother frantically sought Father Feletti (the head of the Dominican Order in Bologna) and begged to keep their child. Their tearful petition was denied by the Chief Inquisitor because his orders had come from the Holy Office in Rome. The next day, as had been commanded, the police came to the Mortara house, and seized the boy. The gendarmes wept, touched by the child's cries and entreaties. Nevertheless, they conscientiously performed their duty. The police tried to quiet Edgardo with sweets and toys, as they tore the mezzuzah from his neck over his tearful protests. He was taken to a Dominican house in Bologna, and then sent to Rome where he was given a new name, Pius, along with his own, during another baptism. Eventually he was sent to the House of Catechumens in Rome where he was educated in the Catholic faith.[1]

The Papal authorities' decision was based on the canon law which stated that a child baptized in the Roman Catholic faith had to be educated as a Christian. Although the church forbade forced baptism of heretics or infidels and their children, that ruling did not apply to a dying person.

Indeed, it was an obligation to baptize the dying unbeliever. In the case of Edgardo, a servant girl, Anna Morisi, illegally employed by the Mortaras,[2] thought the child was dying while she was tending him during an illness. She baptized him, but the child subsequently recovered. Later, she confessed the deed to a Dominican priest who reported the incident to his superiors. Consequently, the child was kidnapped and the order for Edgardo's seizure was upheld by the Holy Congregation. The Mortaras frantically solicited the help of the Piedmontese Jewish community in Turin. Aided by that community the father then traveled throughout western Europe communicating with many Jewish communities who raised funds to assist the family. Through these efforts the case became a "cause celebre" and a source of European agitation and propaganda.[3]

While other Western European states had gradually granted citizenship and some rights to Jews, the Roman States maintained severe barriers to Jewish rights. The Papacy revoked the Napoleonic decrees and nullified the reforms of the Revolution of 1848. Jews were forced to live in a walled Ghetto; they were prohibited from hiring Christian servants and they were excluded from the professions, manufacturing and some businesses. Even Jewish visitors from abroad were allowed to stay only for short periods and were subject to strict surveillance. The police revived the legend of ritual murder at Passover, and frequently kidnapped children who were then raised as Catholics in the House of Catechumens.[4]

The kidnapping in 1858 once more pointed to the precarious status of many Roman Jews. The reaction of the Jewish communities in Western Europe reflected their new confidence as, first in Sardinia-Piedmont, then in the other countries (including the United States), they reacted in a positive fashion to protect themselves from what they considered their dangerous enemy. Despite the differences and animosities which existed between the Jewish groups in the diaspora, they closed ranks in the face of danger to their co-religionists.

Twenty-one Jewish Sardinian congregations addressed an appeal to the London Board of Deputies, representing English Jews, and to the French Central Consistory. Their appeal was addressed to the "Universal Press of the World," and they urged Jews to act saying:

> . . . Such an appeal should naturally come from
> the single corner of Italy in which the toleration of
> conflicting worship is clearly proclaimed. . . . The
> members of the Jewish consistories of France and

England should look upon it as a sacred obligation to make an appeal to their respective governments. We trust their voice will be heard in countries where an enlightened toleration prevails, and that thanks to the interposition of these two nations, the authorities at Rome . . . will no longer . . . trouble the order and peace of Jewish families in the name of a religion which declares itself to be founded on the most solid bases of humanity and fraternal charity.[5]

Through the use of the media, the Sardinian Jewish community was able to mobilize both Jewish and world opinion against the Papal action. French Jews, represented by the Central Israélite Consistory, petitioned Napoleon III to use his influence to persuade the Pope to return Edgardo to his parents.[6] Forty German rabbis, representing many German states, cooperated in sending a joint request to the Pope, not only seeking the restitution of the Mortara child, but also an end to clandestine baptisms and its subsequent abductions.[7] The congregations of Baden concurred, and also sent a petition of protest to the grand-duke of their state.[8] The London Board of Deputies, too, sent a petition to the Pope, as well as one to Lord Malmesbury, Secretary of Foreign Affairs. They also sent notes to Holland and the United States requesting cooperation.[9] The Rabbis of Holland responded by writing a "memorial" in Latin to the Pope, begging for the restoration of the boy.[10]

Prussian Jews sent similar petitions to the Prussian Ambassador at Rome. They concluded their statement with these words: "Excellence, this is no solitary case, it has occurred repeatedly; it is reechoed wherever wise laws do not hold fanaticism in check. . . . We Prussian rabbis have liberty of conscience . . . and our mild and just kings have stopped religious persecution. . . ."[11] American Jews held protest meetings in many cities: Syracuse, Charleston, Philadelphia, Boston, Cincinnati, New York, and even San Francisco. They sent appeals to the President, as well as the Secretary of State, to intercede with the Pope.[12] In France, especially in Paris, Jewish excitement and anger was intense. "All business ceased. They (the Jews) are occupied with nothing but the Mortara Affair. They complain frequently of the lack of action by the French government."[13] After the appeals of British Jews to the Foreign Office, to the Cabinet, and to the Catholic clergy seemed unheard, the London Board of Deputies decided to send a Jewish deputation to Rome (headed by Sir Moses Montefiore) to plead with Pius IX. Indeed, in early 1859 Sir Moses Montefiore went to Rome, where he was denied an audience with the Pope. He did have a long and earnest conversation with Cardinal Antonelli, but his efforts were futile.[14]

In England, the United States, and even in some of the German states, liberal anger was expressed openly and forcefully.[15] The British press, on the whole, represented the Protestant point of view, already antagonistic to the Papacy because of Catholic harassment of Protestants in both France and the Papal States.[16] "The Pope has become the protector of child stealers, and seems to be returning to the days of the dark ages of bigotry and barbarism," they declared.[17] Protest meetings were held in Liverpool, while the Christian Evangelical Alliance, and other Protestant groups issued declarations of support for the Mortara parents.[18] The small minority of English Catholics supported the Church by citing Canon law and by emphasizing that the Mortaras had broken the law by hiring Christian servants.[19]

American newspapers were as interested in the case as those in Europe and their prejudices were often similar. Catholics echoed their English brethren,[20] while Protestants seized the occasion to criticize the Pope. The basic issues, they claimed, were those of human rights which the Pope had violated.[21]

However, both the liberal and Jewish attempts to persuade their various governments to intercede with the Papacy were only partially successful. The American government's position, stated by President Buchanan, reiterated his traditional position: "It is the settled policy of the United States to abstain from all interference . . . as they expect other nations to abstain from all interference in the internal affairs of our country."[22] The Austrian Emperor, Francis Joseph, protested to the Pope, but engaged in no further diplomatic action. He followed this protest by stopping all discussion of the case in the Austrian press.[23] The officials of most German States expressed their dismay at Papal policy, but they had little contact with the Papal States, and therefore, were ineffectual. The British government, while sympathetic to the Mortaras, remained silent; Catholic powers, the minister said, could wield more influence, and France should make the major protest.[24]

In France, however, the situation was very different. The French government was committed to the principle of religious freedom. Its response to the Affair was articulated by the French ambassador who wrote: "It is one of the glorious privileges of our government to be able to extend its help to the religiously oppressed of all countries."[25]   Hence, the government protested to the Papacy claiming that the kidnapping was a denial of the parents' natural rights, and therefore, unjust.   Further, the French urged that "all governments should strive to convince the Pope that the return of the child would be in his (the Pope's) best interests."[26]   The defense of Jewish rights had been established in French diplomacy as a precedent by the episode in 1840, known as the Montel Affair.

Daniel Montel and his wife, French Jews from Nîmes, had been forced to disembark at the Port of Fulminino in the Papal States while traveling because Madame Montel, who was pregnant, had become very seasick. Shortly after, she gave birth to a daughter. Unfortunately the delivery was very difficult and the mid-wife thought the baby was dying. Therefore, unbeknownst to the mother, she baptized her. However, the child recovered, and indeed, thrived. The mid-wife informed her confessor of her action—and he called the authorities. The child was taken from her parents and sent to Rome to be educated in the Catholic faith. At that time, the Roman police faithfully adhered to the Canon law.

Frantically, the Montels sought the assistance of French diplomats. The French Chargé d'Affaires strongly protested the kidnapping of the infant by the police.[27] The French ambassador insisted that because Daniel Montel was a French citizen he must "be treated in the Papal States the same as his compatriots, regardless of differences in religion."[28] The Pope was steadfast and insistent upon the maintenance of the Canon law regarding baptism.   However, he did not wish to offend the French government. Therefore, the Papacy agreed to return the infant to the French ambassador provided that the French government, in turn, would supervise the child's education. The diplomats accepted the child and guaranteed the French government would adhere to Papal demands, provided that Roman stipulations for the child's rearing would not be in violation of the French constitution, which guaranteed freedom of religion. The Holy See did not wish to antagonize the French government, but was equally determined to maintain Canon law. The Pope also understood that the French government would not force its citizens to raise their children in a different faith, nor would the French government separate a family for that purpose. Clearly, each side had been firmly resolute in upholding their most cherished principles. The agreement enabled both parties to save face, and thus satisfied, they quietly resolved the dispute. [29]

In 1858, therefore, moved by this diplomatic precedent and humanitarian interests, the French ambassador strove to alter the Pope's decision regarding the Mortara child. Gramont, the French diplomat described the Mortara parents' grief in minute detail, hoping sympathy would sway Pius IX. Though he was moved by the parents' plight, the Pope continued to insist that: "As head of the Catholic Church he could not push the child back into Judaism. . . ."[30] He declared that he had reached his decision only after much prayer and meditation, and he insisted that providence had intervened directly in this case. Observers noted that Pius IX seemed moved by a kind of Christian fatalism.[31] The Pope remained rigidly uncompromising on what he felt were Catholic principles and law; baptism administered during danger of death was justified, and, therefore, his ruling was religiously proper.[32] The Papacy was fully aware of the sharp criticism directed against its conduct, but the Pope was convinced that Catholic dogma could not be challenged. Critics of the Canon law were wrong, unless they could prove the baptism itself was invalid, or that the servant girl had lied. The Pope would not permit the laws of the Papal States to be contravened.[33]

Most foreign diplomats took little action, but the French were assured of their sympathy. Armed with this knowledge, the French ambassador continued to press his case. Gramont emphasized that the adverse publicity lessened the prestige and respect for the Papacy. Cardinal Antonelli (the Papal Secretary of Foreign Affairs) agreed that the Mortara Affair had produced a loss of support for the Vatican.[34] The Pope was also concerned as Gramont reported that "of all the arguments that I presented to the Pope, the one to which he has been the most sensitive has been the one concerning the rift the Affair has made between Napoleon III and himself."[35] Documents from the Montel Affair were submitted to Antonelli in the hope that the Papacy would find a way to compromise.[36] Unfortunately, unlike the Montels, the Mortaras were Roman citizens. The Pope was obdurate, and the French felt they could not actively interfere in Rome without arousing European suspicions.[37] Though unsuccessful diplomatically, the French government maintained an official position that the kidnapping was a denial of the parents' natural rights and, therefore, unjust.

However, despite the stance of the government, some Catholics in France remained convinced of the sanctity of the Church's position. Among these the most active and influential role was played by a journalist, Louis Veuillot, who was born in 1813, the son of a poor barrel maker. He received a very limited elementary education, and even fewer religious lessons. The poverty of his family necessitated that he work. At age thirteen he was a clerk and messenger boy for a law firm. Gradually, through acquaintance with innumerable literary figures and his own talent, he became a journalist. After visiting Rome in 1839, he converted to Catholicism, abandoning his religious indifference. Henceforth, his devotion to the Papacy became the focus of his philosophy. He eschewed the complexities and subtleties of theological and philosophical thought in favor of absolute and total belief. For Veuillot, all those who denied the truth of *his* faith were spiritually inferior, and those who rejected his God should, at the least, be forced to lead a moral life.[38] Conservative in his political attachments, in 1851 he supported Louis Napoleon in the belief that the new Emperor would defend Catholic interests. He became embroiled in bitter feuds with the liberal Catholics and emerged as the ardent champion of ultramontane orthodox Catholicism, defender of the Pope and embattled antagonist of the revolution.[39] His newspaper, *L'Univers,* became the vehicle through which he expressed his ideas and advanced his principles. Veuillot alarmed many moderate Catholics, who rightly feared that his intransigence would arouse anticlericalism. The position he took on the Mortara Affair also marked the first open breach in the uneasy alliance between the ultramontane church and the state.

From the start, *L'Univers* endorsed the Papal position and ardently defended the Vatican's decision regarding the Mortara child. Veuillot's arguments, though seemingly cruel and quasi-medieval, were rigidly logical once one accepted the basic premise.[40] The most important object in every man's existence, argued Veuillot, was the salvation of the soul as a means of attaining everlasting life. Only the Roman Catholic church, through her teachings, could provide grace. Therefore, if the child had been baptized, it was morally indefensible to permit him to return to eternal damnation. Though the father's natural rights were important, the spiritual welfare of the child was paramount. The church's position therefore took precedence over the natural rights of the parents. Hence the Papacy had acted wisely and justly in removing the child from his parents' custody, since it had thereby saved his eternal soul. Veuillot further noted that, according to Canon law, adults can never be baptized without their consent, but that a child of an infidel or a Jew in danger of death and baptized without his parents' consent must be raised as a Christian, because the child's soul must be protected from the influence of his family. Therefore, the youngster should be educated in a wholesome environment. He further insisted that two rights were being debated: the parents' obligation to decide how their child was to be educated, and the advantages now available to the child through his baptism. The parents' rights were a part of the natural law; the child's belonged to the supernatural. Though all rights come from God—in this case supernatural rights were superior and deserved to triumph: "It was God's will. . . ."[41]

Veuillot became the most vocal, redoubtable and untroubled defender of the Vatican's moral position in this case.[42] He characterized all the newspapers which attacked the Papacy as either revolutionary or Voltairian. He continued:

> . . .They have used the child as means of under-
> mining the church. The attempt of the govern-
> ment to exercise diplomatic pressure is wrong.
> The French can not interfere in the internal affairs
> of another sovereign state without creating an in-
> ternational crisis, and there are more important
> events than a Jew's fate in Bologna. We have been
> accused of moving back to the Middle Ages . . .
> but it is you who are becoming pagan. . . . This
> child has been touched by the Divine. You wish
> to safeguard liberty of conscience for a Jewish
> father, but you would sacrifice the same liberty for
> the Christian child. . . .The poor little Mortara boy
> has been granted a marvelous opportunity: the
> privilege of a Catholic education. Nothing more
> indicates the decline of religion than the furor over
> the baptism of the young Mortara. . . . In the past
> Christians would have accepted the Papal deci-
> sion; now the same people criticize his action. A
> revolution in values and beliefs has shaken mod-
> ern society and pagan prejudices have taken pre-
> cedence over the eternal verities.[43]

There were other ultramontane papers which sustained Veuillot's ideas, but none of the others were as vehement or strident as L'Univers. Le Monde and L'Union essentially repeated the same arguments, but in restrained and more carefully moderated tones. The Journal de Bruxelles offered a strange rationale which was coopted by some of the French Catholic press. That paper claimed that the child, aged seven, although taken to Rome, was not separated from his family. The father could follow the child, and visit him regularly so that the family ties would remain unbroken. " Force," they claimed, "was not used to impose the new faith upon the child. . . ." Edgar had accepted Christianity with spontaneity and a genuine "grace of spirit. . . ."[44] The Abbé Pelletier of Orleans attempted to rationalize the seizure of the child in even more conciliatory terms:

> All civilized countries and their legislatures have not uniformly resolved questions of individual liberty, paternal and marital rights, nor the authority of guardianship. Therefore, there are bound to be differing views, according to the varying perceptions or rationales of individuals. To those who did not value baptism, and who did not believe Catholicism superior to other educations, the actions of the Pope seem frivolous. They are free to demur and to hold their prejudices, but so are those who believe in baptism and in the superiority of Christianity.[45]

Most of the provincial press did not adopt the ultramontane ideas. The few that did were *Le Courrier de Lyon, Ésperance de Nancy, Ésperance de Nantes* and the *Journal de l'Ain*. *Le Courrier de Lyon* stressed the fact that the Mortara family employed a Christian servant, forbidden by a law (humane in the eyes of the church), which was passed expressly to prevent such clandestine baptisms.[46] *L' Alsacien,* another provincial paper, complained that the sudden concern for the Mortara child was simply a veiled attack against the Holy Church by the Left. No doubt some felt genuine sympathy for the Mortara family, the paper said. However, it went on, others both in Paris and in the provinces used the sad fate of this family to give vent to their petty political and religious passions.[47]

The rest of the Catholic press differed in its support of the Papacy. Indeed, some Catholics, like the writer Forcade, were confused about the conflict between paternal rights supported by the Church itself and the spiritual authority of the dogma.[48] To Forcade, the kidnapping of a child was "contrary to moral law, and contrary to the civil law in both France and England." He did not challenge the religious dogma, but he regarded the Papal decision as a damaging political act. The Mortara kidnapping led to a conflict between the moral, human, and Catholic law; even worse it had led to a diminishing respect in Europe for the Holy Pontiff.[49]

Le *Journal des Débats* insisted that the child's seizure was a crime committed under the French flag which floated over Rome. "It is under the protection of our arms that good sense and humanity has been abused," the paper noted.[50] In a series of three prominently placed letters, Abbé Delacouture, a Gallican priest, stoutly defended the natural rights of the parents to raise their child. He cited Canon law and theological opinion to contradict *L'Univers*. Baptism conferred on a child without a parent's permission violated the natural law, clearly a contravention of Catholic dogma. He quoted Benedict XIV's Bull which stated that dependent children are subject to their parents. "Thus the natural law is inviolable and religion can never challenge it. . . ."[51] These articles were later expanded and published as a brochure which enjoyed a tremendous sale. The Gallican Abbé criticized not only the actions of the Pontifical government but also challenged the writers and the editors of the *L'Univers* who, he claimed, "knew no moderation in their opinions or in their language."[52]

The semi-official press criticized the seizure of non-Catholic children in somewhat muted tones. The language of these papers remained for the most part measured and circumspect. Typical of this approach was the statement in the *Constitutionnel*: "The French government profoundly regrets the conduct pursued by the court of Rome . . . and the French ambassador has, from the first, used every effort to enlighten the Holy See as to its consequences, and show it that French public opinion would deplore an act which violated the most sacred affection."[53] Such circumspection would become more difficult as Veuillot's polemic became more shrill.

The anticlerical papers, on the other hand, seized the Mortara Affair as the proof of the dangers of ultramontane Catholicism, and engaged in a bitter debate with Veuillot and his allies. Guéroult, in *La Presse*, noted with asperity how fanatical the ultramontanes were.[54] *Siècle* pointed out the inconsistencies between natural law and canon law. The Papal government was an example of the "ancien regime," which denied human rights of individuals and negated the values promulgated by the French revolution. Having declared that the French government should prevent the consummation of such an injustice by the Vatican, especially since the Pope owed his temporal power to the military intervention of France: "All friends of humanity, progress, and civilization must hope this appeal will be heard, and those of you who know the Emperor's sense of justice and fair play are certain that it will not have been made in vain."[55] *Charivari* published a satirical article on the affair which was as biting as the open attacks of the anticlerical papers.[56] The majority of the provincial papers tended to remain neutral or reprinted the articles of the government or the anticlerical press.

Brochure literature joined in attacking the ultramontane position. One writer characterized Veuillot as "the Polignac of Catholicism" and criticized the Papacy itself:

> . . . Any country, no matter which one, in which law is still subordinate to theology, that nation remains outside civilization, and its laws ought to be modified. . . . The unity of the temporal and spiritual power is not an inalienable right. It may be a good political manoeuvre to maintain the Pope's secular prerogatives— but it is a *political* act only. . . . The Papal States should be reformed by the introduction of the Napoleonic Code.[57]

Veuillot soon found himself a minority voice with minimal support both in the provinces and in Paris,[58] as most churchmen preferred a politic silence rather than open agreement with Veuillot. His arguments had swayed very few who were not deeply committed to his position. He agreed with those who accused him of being both medieval and fanatical, accepting these descriptive terms as a badge of honor. His opponents, he thundered, had adopted paganism which was the real meaning of secularism. The principles of religious toleration were erroneous. The anger of the Jews, along with the concurrence of the Protestants, revealed that both these groups were, in fact, essentially pagan.

Thus the arguments and polemics raged in the press. The citations of canon law, the recitation of the natural and civil rights, revealed the chasm of the unyielding claims which divided the two sides. They were irreconcilable and uncompromising. Those who were opposed to the Church saw in the events and in the arguments of *L'Univers* an affirmation of their suspicions that the church threatened the family authority structure and individual rights. Through the sacrament of penance the Church could interfere in marriage relationships and other personal affairs. The Catholic schools would, through their influence and teaching, overrule the parents' authority. The Mortara Affair clearly illustrated, at least to most anticlericals, the validity of their deepest suspicions and fears: the threat to liberty.[59] For the ultramontanes the enemy was secularism and religious toleration, those forces which would undermine traditional Catholic institutions and influence in both the state and the schools. Gradually the issues began to transcend the tragedy of the Mortara family itself and to assume more ideological ramifications.

Though Veuillot was not certain of public reaction he must have sensed both from the lack of press support and the cautious silence of many churchmen that the large part of public opinion was not sympathetic to his position. In general, the public identified with the Mortara parents' grief. They were not interested in either the dogma or the ideology involved in the discussions of the case. In those areas where ultramontane influence was strongest, sympathy for the parents was not as evident, but observers noted that even among the most devout some emotion was expressed for the Mortaras.[60] In Paris and the surrounding areas, where emerging anti-clericalism was stronger, feelings were sharply antagonistic to the church. The working classes, traditionally suspicious of the religious, were permanently alienated from the Church. As one commentator said: "What is so bad is that the odiousness of the Affair falls on the Pope. . . ." Public opinion thus condemned the ultramontanes, especially the priests who seemed to automatically support the canon law.[61] In Besançon, where religious feelings ran deep, it was reported that the Mortara case had a bad effect among the middle classes and the general population.[62] In neighboring Jura, the circulation of La Presse and Siècle suddenly rose sharply (especially in the villages) primarily because of their anticlerical opinions. Many Catholics had difficulty understanding how the canon law could be so rigid and so cruel.[63] Antipathy toward Papal policy on family rights led also to sudden expressions of approbation for the government's administrative changes in Algeria which emphasized religious toleration.[64] The Catholic hierarchy, including even the more moderate Dupanloup, supported the Church on most issues: namely the concept of special privilege, and the exclusiveness of the Roman rite. But many, aware of the deep sympathy of their parishioners to the Mortara parents, were hesitant to aver their support of the Pope too loudly. They were quite rightly concerned over the effects of the Affair on the public and over the widespread disapproval of the press. That did not mean the clergy denied the Vatican's logic, nor were they willing to defend vociferously the government position. Instead, many preferred discretion.[65] However, in those Catholic schools largely supervised by the ultramontanes, Veuillot's arguments, which had been appropriated by the Papacy, were written in simple language and distributed to the schoolchildren.[66] These lessons stressed the importance of the Catholic religion as the only means of salvation, that the church could not sacrifice the sacrament of baptism for the rights of the parents, and that the Mortaras had disobeyed the law by hiring a Christian servant.67

Hence, Veuillot found himself relatively isolated in a debate that revealed the unyielding nature of the claims on both sides. Feeling on the defensive, angered by the resistance of the moderate Catholics, and alarmed by the paucity of overt support, he slowly began to inject the poison of antisemitism into the debates. First he identified those who denied his arguments as either pagan or irreligious—those on the left who subscribed to the principles of 1789. Some of those who protested the Mortara abduction, he declared, were connected with Mazzinian radicals who were using the Affair as a "means of furthering their subversive views." Those Jews and Protestants who were the most enthusiastic in their support of such dangerous ideas were heretics and infidels. That argument has, at least, a modicum of truth. "The sensation which this affair has caused in the Jewish and heretical press does not astonish us. . . .Their writers scarcely believed in the existence of God and deny the whole system of Christianity, and thus revolt against the sacred right exercised by the Holy Church . . . ," he wrote. Veuillot was particularly incensed by the world-wide protest against the Church. He claimed that it was the Jews, aided by the revolutionary press, that had created the furor. He attacked the *Constitutionnel*, whose publisher, Mirès, was Jewish, as a tool of the "House of Jacob," despite the fact that its writers were Catholic and included the son-in-law of Jean Mocquard, the Emperor's private secretary. The agents of Mazzini, he continued, determined to wound the Papacy, were financed by Jews. "Everywhere that eastern race rules supreme. They have purchased the copyright of all the important newspapers in Europe: the *Times*, *Constitutionnel*, *Débats*, etc. . . ."68

The semiofficial *Constitutionnel* responded with angry phrases, abandoning its early restraint. "There is a journal . . . that has scandalized the great majority of Roman Catholics. . . . It designates as revolutionists all who do not defend religion in its own manner. For our own part, we will say with full conviction to the writers of the *Univers* who call their contemporaries Mazzinians: 'Mazzini is the scourge of Italy, and you are the Mazzini of the Church!'" Thus that paper condemned the continuing invectives of Veuillot and company.69 This editorial in the *Constitutionnel* was followed by an announcement that Prince Napoleon, Minister for Algerian Affairs, had appointed a few Jews to the local colonial councils, because "in the presence of the various forms of worship practised in Algeria, it is useful and advisable to show . . . that freedom of religion is absolute and complete before our laws."[70] Veuillot was especially irritated by the official proclamation that all religions were equal before the law and that freedom of religion must be absolute. Since he believed Jews were mainly responsible for the continuing criticism of the Papacy, he proceeded to launch a series of vicious attacks upon them. He used his paper, *L'Univers*, as a forum where he exposed the operations, beliefs, customs, and prejudices of the Jews. Guided by a Jewish convert named Drack,[71] Veuillot proceeded to demonstrate the falseness of Jewish Talmudic teachings. He also attacked Jewish writers such as Solomon Cahen, J. Cahen, Simon Bloch and Alexandre Weill, along with others whom he suspected of being philosemites: Havin, Plée, Guéroult, Paradol, Alloury, and especially the Abbé Delacouture.[72]

Veuillot accused Jews of being both conspiratorial revolutionaries undermining the Pope's temporal power, and international bankers seeking world domination. He claimed that their ethnic culture provided them with characteristics which prevented them from ever being assimilated: thus he insisted Jews could never be Frenchmen! Moreover, the Talmud preached lies and commanded Jews to hate Christians.[73]

Ultimately, Veuillot's charges and accusations provoked a strong Jewish response. Alexandre Weill, in a long brochure, castigated Veuillot for his fanaticism, his bigotry, and especially his misinformation. In language which was by turns witty, clever, and amusing, Weill accused Veuillot of lacking knowledge of Hebrew, of not reading the Talmud, and above all, of being ignorant of Biblical lore. To Veuillot, claimed Weill, Protestants represented the cause of evil among men, a force which had corrupted human beings. However, the Catholic world that existed in the Middle Ages was as evil, corrupt, bellicose, and power-hungry as our own. He reminded Veuillot that the apostles were all Jews and that Jesus did not come from Gascony, Lorraine, or Franche-Compte, but from Judea. As to the question of conversion, Weill noted that if Veuillot and his supporters had shown more humanity, charity and sympathy in their behavior in keeping with Christian teaching, all would acquiesce in their truths. "But as you (Veuillot) are not better, nor more loving, nor more charitable towards men, nor more zealous in fulfilling your duties than I, what exigency moves me to leave my religion for yours . . . ?" he queried.[74]

Another critic, Rabbi Astruc, attacked Veuillot's ignorance of the Talmud. The Talmud was not absolute law, as Veuillot believed, but a collection of commentaries, anecdotes, and analysis of law which helped Jews understand the Bible. What Veuillot assumed to be derogations of other faiths were instead reflections of the Jewish belief in their own truths. Further, in view of Veuillot's polemics and in the light of Christian behavior in the past, there was little reason for Jews to love their persecutors. "No, Jews do not hate Christians," Rabbi Astruc noted, "they love them when they deserve it."[75]

However, Veuillot's editorial, which revived the "blood libel," was the final act which aroused the united ire of the Jewish community and inspired them to take some concerted action against *L'Univers*. Veuillot had expressed his anger against government policy as follows:

> If they (Jews) blaspheme Christ over the cradles of their children, if in the distant countries where they have fallen below the lowest barbarian there is a necessity for their Passover . . . the blood of a Christian child . . . in order that having crucified the lamb they may devour it (him) in those who have become his flesh—what else have we to do but to follow the example of the great sacrifice and return them good for evil. But I do not wish that any good is done to this people on the one hand by multiplying the privileges of this detestable industry, and on the other, by lavishing on it political favors which only encourage its natural insolence.[76]

The reassertion of the blood libel with its roots in a long buried medieval past, revived painful collective memories of massacres, persecutions and death. Reaction was expressed throughout France by the various provincial consistories. The Jews of Nancy characterized Veuillot's articles as: "A monstrous attack of hate against our cult."[77] "The Jewish population of Haut Rhin, more exposed than others to violence, have been very upset. . . ." Others characterized Veuillot's journalism as an "odious attack against Judaism . . ." and expressed the hope that justice would put an end to "this insolent and provocative polemic. . . ."[78] The Central Israélite Consistory responded with alacrity, and issued a protest the day after the article appeared. Veuillot's attack and a similar article in *L'Union* were specifically singled out for complaint. The Consistory claimed that these articles were defamatory and preached "scorn and hate against a class of citizens . . . and also noted that the *L'Union* article was as detestable as that of *L'Univers*. They also felt that the articles were unjust and should be suppressed.[79] However, no *avertissement* was actually issued. Indeed rumors abounded that Prince Napoleon himself requested that punishment be suspended against Veuillot.[80] Although government officials were appalled at Veuillot's harangue, they refrained from action ostensibly because the government did not wish to interfere in a "religious matter." As an alternative, the minister suggested that perhaps a civil suit would stifle Veuillot.[81] Closer to the truth, perhaps, was the fact that the debate had become too heated and a fear arose that Veuillot's demagoguery dangerously stimulated legitimist feeling in France. Moreover, the government was surreptitiously preparing for the Italian war and was fearful of an open attack in December 1858 on the leading ultramontane paper. Instead a directive was issued terminating all discussion of the Mortara Affair.

The Central Israélite Consistory decided to institute a libel suit against *L'Univers* and received the necessary permission from the government.[82] Indeed, rumors spread that the government had instigated the consistory to sue so that the ultramontanes could be prosecuted without involving official action.[83] Adolph Crémieux and Eugene Bethmont, attorneys engaged for the case, proved to be less than enthusiastic. They argued that legal technicalities might lead to the loss of their case. They further insisted that: "In a trial for defamation, there would be little publicity, no accounts in the newspapers, and a small audience in the court. Little would be gained in refuting Veuillot's lies." They asked a rhetorical question: Is this (1858) the proper time to institute such an action? "The entire press . . . revealed the most noble and universal sympathy in favor of the sanctity of the home and the sacred right of paternal authority. . . ."[84] The Central Consistory wavered and then decided against the suit. It withdrew the legal complaints against Veuillot and *L'Univers*.[85]

Although some Jews were discouraged by their failure to rectify the injustice of the Mortara kidnapping, and were disturbed by the terrible conditions which plagued Roman Jews, others saw in the Affair evidences of a new spirit. As a Jewish commentator observed: "Who would have fifty years ago noticed this affair? Who would have raised his voice in favor of a poor hard working Israelite? Now, on the contrary there has been a loud and vehement outcry, and the press criticism has been accompanied by the protests of governments. Let us beware of despairing, let us have confidence in our right, confidence especially in public opinion. . . . The Papacy has been stigmatized, and the cause of the Mortara family has gained world sympathy." But, putting self congratulations aside, Jews saw clearly their weakness in being able to redress wrongs.[86]

American Jewry was concerned over its inability to effect any real political influence in the United States; English and French Jews were also aware of their political impotence, and began to discuss the need to develop a means of international cooperation. The British Jews were more optimistic in their assessment of the situation. They were well aware that no government could make the Pope change his decision and that the English foreign ministry would not act alone. Even though Jews had failed to rectify a major wrong, some good had emerged. One editor commented, "Within the community this atrocity has once more moved the sections of Israel to cooperate and this contributed towards accustoming them in emergencies to look to each other for the necessary support." He went further, observing that if Jews learned to work together in the face of common danger they might also learn to function together to accomplish daily positive goals.[87]

French Jews, however, were not as sanguine. France was Catholic and ultramontane opinion not only supported the Pope, but *L'Univers* had indulged in antisemitic polemics.[88] One writer counseled his readers that public opinion will gradually forget this crisis and turn to other subjects. "The Mortara Affair," Cahen noted, "lays bare ultramontane tendencies; it shows the extent of what you have to fear; let it be your signal of alarm!" He suggested that a central organization should be created in Paris to which Jews throughout the free countries would send contributions and delegates. The danger for Jews in the Mortara Affair appeared in the arguments sustained by the ultramontanes in support of the Papacy;[89] for it was an "attack on freedom of religion in France . . . and an attack on the rights of the family, security, honor, liberty, that threatens the life of men."[90] The concept of a centralized international organization to combat antisemitism and defend Jewish welfare had surfaced among young French intellectuals as early as the 1830s. It had been frequently mentioned in the Jewish press; "it is urgent that western Jewry assist their brothers in the east" (1844), and again in 1845, "we must utilize all the means at our disposal to help our co-religionists acquire complete civil and political equality in the whole world."[91] Jewish leadership had been frequently solicited to form such a group, but the proposal never crystallized. In 1851 Jules Carvallo (a young Saint-Simonian entrepreneur) suggested that French Jews seize the initiative in organizing an international congress of Jews to help their co-religionists achieve equality, but to no avail. It was the example of an English Christian group in 1855, the Universal Evange- ical Alliance, devoted to missionary efforts among youth, especially Jew- ish adolescents, that again aroused Jews to action. Isadore Cahen, in the *Archives Israélites,* responded by demanding that Jews follow this example and form their own Jewish alliance to teach, to defend their interests, to cement the ties among various Jewish communities, and to give "mutual assistance" to those Jews in need.[92]

The Mortara Affair alerted the Jewish community to its precarious position and the need for international cooperation. Therefore, acting upon these assumptions, a group of prominent Jews in Paris in 1860 formed an organization to cope with local and international problems. They called themselves the Alliance Israélite Universelle. Almost all the leaders and founders of this group were laymen: and the Alliance, devoted to Jewish causes, remained entirely secular. The goals of the Alliance were directed to achieve the "emancipation and spiritual progress of the Jews," to assist all Jews who were being persecuted, and to help establish publications to aid in these tasks.[93] Initially the Alliance had been organized to combat religious persecution, but rapidly converted its main efforts into educa- tional activities.[94] The Alliance's first efforts were to seek rectification for the Mortara family; its leaders petitioned Victor-Emanuel for assistance, but, as with every other effort, this proved fruitless, too.[95] Despite the failure in the Mortara Affair, the united effort of the Jewish communities had demonstrated the effectiveness of cooperation in using mass media to communicate their case to governments, and to other communities.

However the stress on cooperation between Jews, especially those of England and the United States, paradoxically seemed to confirm the stereotypes so vividly portrayed by Veuillot, who had spoken so casually of the international conspiracy of the press and the Jews. Many years later Drumont would single out the Alliance Israelite Universelle in *La France Juive* as an international organization through which Jews planned to gain world ascendency.[96]

Louis Veuillot and his antisemitic attacks could not be considered insignificant, as Zeldin claimed, because Veuillot revealed "extraordinary misapprehensions and ignorance" about Jews and Judaism.[97] Indeed, his defense and his arguments defaming Jews were sustained, supported, and even quoted by the Vatican's official and semiofficial press. Catholic antisemitism and approbation gave Veuillot the influence which he could exert upon the ultramontane and legitimist movements in France. The Jes- uit paper *Cattolica Civiltà* published a long and very detailed explanation of Papal policy on the Mortara case. In the course of its arguments the paper employed Veuillot's phrases to cite the "Jewish conspiracy to discredit the Papacy," through their world-wide control of the press.[98] The *Giornale Officiale di Roma* published a direct quotation from an article signed by Gueranger. The reprint was inserted "with a distressing authority whose only aim was to offend as much as to convince. "[99] It was obvious to all that Veuillot was considered the official champion of the Church's interest; his antisemitism was a part of the religious, traditional antisemitic sentiments sustained by the Church itself throughout the nineteenth century.[100]

Debates in the French press over the importance of Veuillot in the Catholic schema attested to his influence. Journalists commented on how much esteem he enjoyed among the French clergy, and noted that *L'Univers* took a position denying religious freedom, a posture supported to a large degree by the French Church.[101] "The connection that some have attempted to attribute to *L'Univers* and the Holy See, does not exist," claimed the *Ami de la Religion* (a liberal Catholic paper). The *Courrier de Paris* responded immediately: "There is unfortunately between the acts of the Roman Church and the theories of the *Univers* such an identity that it is impossible not to recognize the connection . . . which exists between them."[102] The fact that *L'Univers* could arouse such debate was eloquent testimony to the paper's importance.

Some French clergy disapproved of the tone of Veuillot's opposition, and many were alienated by his attacks on modernity. The Bishop of Mans, Msgr. Manquette, wrote to Veuillot: "I consider your article (on the Affair) an act of treason toward the Church."[103] But such men were definitely in the minority, since the majority of the French bishops and clergymen gave Veuillot quiet unqualified praise and adulation. The letters he kept from prominent churchmen were historical testimony both to his influence and the respectability of the antisemitism that he preached. Pius IX had already indicated his approval in his official newspaper, but he went even further. He instructed the Papal Nuncio to inform Veuillot of his warm gratitude for his spirited defense. Msgr. Parisis, Bishop of Arras, wrote to Veuillot on 20 November 1858, on the subject of both religious liberty and the young Edgardo. "The campaign against the official policy of the Prince-Minister (Prince Napoleon) was very bold and at first, I worried because I knew the cousin's character, and he would not permit such criticism, without seeking imperial vengeance." Happily that did not occur. The bishop added that he applauded the journalist's courage and style. "I am happy and proud . . ." he continued, "You alone, in *L'Univers*, have strongly and firmly defended our rights in the case of the small Mortara."[104] R. P. Félix, the eminent Jesuit, praised Veuillot's support of the Church, especially the articles on the Mortara Affair. "They are clear, firm, courageous, Christian, apostolic, and eloquent. . . ."[105] The Bishop of Beauvais, Msgr. Gignoux, was so impressed with Veuillot's journalism that he attempted to pressure the newspapers of his diocese to reprint those articles, but to no avail. Opinion in his parish was adamantly opposed to Veuillot's arguments and were sympathetic to family rights.[106] At no time in his rhetoric was Louis Veuillot ever a racist in the modern sense. He was, nevertheless, antisemitic, if that term implies a dislike for Jews and a disrespect for their beliefs. Indeed, this was how he described his feeling in response to the accusation that he wished to exterminate Jews:

> We are enemies of Judaism and of Jewry without
> being (an enemy) of the Jews. We have preserved
> them in spite of our Christian antipathy, for we are
> Christian. We do not wish liberty for the children
> of Abraham, although we wish them to become
> our brothers. We do not want to treat them badly,
> only that they must truly free themselves by aban-
> doning Judaism, and the Talmud, and the Book of
> the Rabbis, for the Bible, the book of God. That is
> where we must lead them.[107]

Veuillot's arguments over Edgar's baptism had been stifled by the government's directives, but his venomous attacks upon Jewry were not so easily silenced. The Jewish community would have to confront his continued expletives throughout 1859. As for the fate of the young Edgar Mortara, he remained in the House of Catechumens, where he was thoroughly indoctrinated in the Catholic faith. Contemporary accounts recorded a passive, withdrawn, quiet child who was unusually obedient.[108] He exhibited a great facility for foreign languages, which served him well when he became a priest in a religious order. Whether "the child . . . himself was actually thankful for what the nursemaid and priest had done,"[109] is immaterial. The Mortara family was distraught, the father's business ruined, the mother left heartbroken, and parents and siblings were forever separated.[110] The monk, Edgardo, left Italy and lived in Poitiers, France after 1870, where he remained until his death in 1940.

Failure to return Edgar to his parents and the suppression of newspaper articles did not end the discussion or the antisemitic rhetoric of the ultramontane press. The Affair's significance lay far beyond the fate of an obscure boy, for it was analogous to the Dreyfus Affair, both in the nature of the passionate debates, and the ideological cleavages that were revealed and indeed, left unhealed. The episode also aroused enormous emotional reaction throughout the world reflecting the interest in the relationships between the church and state, and family rights versus religious law. The Mortara Affair was also important in French foreign policy because French troops protected the Pope's temporal power in Rome, and the scandal inadvertently became entangled in the long and bitter arguments over the Roman Question.

The discussions evoked by the description of the case in the media transcended the fate of the participants. Because the ideological considerations were of universal application, they contained a relevance that was apparent in the political developments in France prior to World War II; moreover, its echoes were heard in the Beekman and Finaly episodes of 1953,[111] an indication perhaps that the implication of the Affair extended well into the modern era.

Moreover, the Affair revealed the basic antagonisms that existed between the government and conservatives on human rights and freedom of conscience. The emperor had suppressed the debates over Edgar Mortara because he did not wish the issue to further divide France, as he was preparing a foreign policy that presaged even more strident discord. This new controversy was precipitated in July 1858 when Napoleon III met Cavour at Plombières and plotted the unification of Italy. As the political events in Italy threatened the Pope's temporal power, the debates among the French clergy became even more frenzied.

---

[1] The best and most complete account is in Gemma Volli, *Il casa Mortara nel primo centenario*, (Rome: La Rassegna Mensile di Israel, 1960); Report of the Vice consul of Ancona to Lyons, 22 September 1858, Public Record Office, MSS. London Foreign Office (hereafter referred to as PRO, FO, 197/25.

[2] The Jews of Nancy. Jews were forbidden to hire Christian servants in the Roman States.

[3] Volli, 13-14.

[4] Cecil Roth, *History of the Jews of Italy*, (Philadelphia: Jewish Publication Society of America, 1946), 470-73; Mario Rossi, "Emancipation of the Jews in Italy," in Duker and Ben Horin (eds.), *Emancipation and Counter-Emancipation*, 224-25.

[5] *Jewish Chronicle*, (London), 19 September 1858 translated the protest from *La Presse*, 3 September 1858; c. f. *L'Univers Israélite*, October 1858; *Morning Herald*, (London), 13 September 1858; *Morning Advertiser*, (London), 2 September 1858.

[6] L'Affaire Mortara, Dossier M, III, Archives of the Central Israelite Consistory, Paris, MSS (hereafter referred to as ACIC); *Jewish Chronicle*, (London), 17 September 1858; *L'Univers Israélite*, October 1858; *Archives Israélites*, October 1858.

[7] *Jewish Chronicle*, (London), 15 October 1858.

[8] Ibid., January 1858.

[9] Ibid., 22 October 1858.

[10] *Archives Israélites*, October 1858.

[11] *Jewish Chronicle*, (London), 15 October 1858.

[12] Bertram Korn, *The American Reaction to the Mortara Case*, (Cincinnati: American Archives, 1957), 20-35, 126.

[13] Report to Gramont on the state of public opinion, Paris, 19 October 1858, Archives du Ministère des Affaires étrangères, MSS, Paris, Correspondance Politique, Rome (hereafter referred to as AMAE, CP).

[14] *Jewish Chronicle*, (London), 12 November, 22 October 1858; 4, 25 March; 22, 29 April; 13 May 1859; Letter of Moses Montefiore, M III, Affaire Mortara ACIC; Moses and Lady Montefiore, *Diaries*, (Chicago, 1890), II, 82-92, 95-99.

[15] *Der Israelitischen Volkslehrer*, (Frankfurt am Main), 14, 21 October 1858; *American Israélite*, 14 October 1858.

[16] *Guardian*, (London), 20 October 1858.

[17] *Morning Herald*, (London), 19 October 1858.

[18] Ibid.

[19] *Jewish Chronicle*, (London), 20, 23, 26 October 1858, cited in the Catholic papers *Kent*, *Beacon*, and *Globe*.

[20] Howard Marraro, *American Opinion on the Unification of Italy*, (New York: Columbia Univ. Press, 1932), 151-52.

[21] Ibid.

[22] Cyrus Adler and Aaron Margolith, *With Firmness on the Right: American Diplomatic Action Affecting Jews*, 1840-1945, (New York: American Jewish Committee, 1946), xxvii.

[23] *Archives Israélites*, October 1858.

[24] Cowley to Malmesbury, Paris, 30 September 1858, PRO, FO, 519/19.

[25] Gramont to Walewski, Rome, 25 July 1858, Archives du Ministère des Affaires étrangères, Correspondance politique (hereafter referred to as AMAE, CP).

[26] Walewski to Gramont, Biarritz, 22 September 1858; Gramont to Walewski, Rome, 5 October 1858, AMAE, CP.; Cowley to Malmesbury, Paris, 30 September 1858, PRO, FO 519/19; Villamarina to Cavour, 21 November 1858 in *Il Carteggio Cavour-Nigra dal 1858 al 1861*, (Bologna: A cura della R. Commissione editrice, 1926-1929), I, 206-07.

[27] Rayneval to Thiers, Rome, 26 June 1840, AMAE, CP.

[28] Ibid.

[29] Foreign Office to Rayneval, Paris, 8 July 1840; Cardinal Lambruschini to Rayneval, Rome, 26 June 1840; Rayneval to Thiers, Rome, 18 July 1840; Rayneval to Louis-Phillippe, Rome, 23 July 1840, AMAE, CP. This correspondence was reproduced in A. Weil, "Un precedent de 'L'Affaire Mortare,'" *Revue historique*, (May 1921): 49-65; c. f. Jules Isaac, *L'Affaire Finaly*, (Marseilles; Editions du Circle intellectual pour le rayonnement de la pensée et de la culture juive, 1953), 20.

[30] Villamarina to Cavour, 21 November 1858, CCN, I, 206-08; Gramont to Walewski, 5 October 1858, AMAE, CP; Cowley to Malmesbury, 13 October 1858, Paris, PRO, FO, 519/19.

[31] Gramont to Walewski, Rome, 8 October 1858, AMAE, CP.

[32] Gramont to Walewski, 30 November 1858, AMAE, CP.

[33] Ibid., Gramont to Walewski, Rome, 30 October 1858, AMAE, CP.

[34] *Manchester Guardian*, 24 November 1858 reported a letter written by Antonelli which stated: "I hope you do my common sense the honor to believe that I judge the Mortara Affair as you do; an unmistakable blunder. . . ."; c. f. Cowley to Malmesbury, Paris, 13 October 1858, PRO, FO 519/19.

[35] Gramont to Walewski, Rome, 18, 30 October 1858, AMAE, CP.

[36] Gramont to Walewski, Rome, 30 November 1858, AMAE, CP.

[37] Walewski to Gramont, Biarritz, 22 September 1858, AMAE, CP.

[38] Waldemar Gurian, "Louis Veuillot," *Catholic Historical Review*, 36 (1951): 385-89.

[39] Marvin L. Brown, *Louis Veuillot*, (Durham, North Carolina: Moore, 1977). This is one of the few biographies in English that is based on archival sources. However, Veuillot's role in the Mortara Affair and his antisemitism are not treated in detail and lacks meaningful discussion.

[40] Pierre de La Gorce, *Histoire du Second Empire*, (Paris, 1894-1905), II, 365.

[41] *L'Univers*, 22, 24 October 1858. Most of the articles in the paper were reproduced in *Louis Veuillot*, Second Series, (Paris: P. Lethielleux, 1925), V, 4-316. Some of these articles were written in collaboration with other journalists: Dom Gueranger, Du Lac, and Coquille.

[42] La Gorce, II, 366.

[43] *L'Univers*, 23, 24, 25 October 1858.

[44] *Journal de Bruxelles*, 18 September 1858 cited in *Archives Israélites*, September 1858.

[45] *L'Univers*, 23 October 1858.

[46] Ibid., 23, 24, 25 October 1858.

[47] Ibid., 27 October 1858.

[48] La Gorce, II, 336.

[49] *Revue des deux Mondes*, 18, (15 November 1858), 218-21.

[50] *Journal des Débats*, 29 September 1858.

[51] Ibid.

[52] Abbé Delacouture, *Le droit canon et le droit naturel dans l'Affaire Mortara*, (Paris, 1858).

[53] *Le Constitutionnel*, 17 October 1858.

[54] R. Rémond, *L'anti-cléricalisme en France de 1815 à nos jours*, (Paris: Fayard, 1976), 63; *La Presse* reprinted in *L'Univers Israélite*, October 1858.

[55] *Le Siècle*, 19, 20 October 1858.

[56] *Charivari*, 3 September 1858, reprinted in *Archives Israélites*, October 1858.

[57] Jules Assézat, *Affaire Mortara, le droit du père*, (Paris, 1858), 19-24.

[58] *Morning Advertiser*, (London), 21 October 1858; Prefect and Procureurs reports indicate the same attitudes.

[59] Rémond, 62-63.

[60] Procureur Report, 29 October 1858, Haut Saone, AN, BB30, 373.

[61] Report on public opinion, Paris, 18 October 1858, AMAE, CP.

[62] Procureur report, 29 November 1858, Besançon, AN, BB30, 373.

[63] Prefect report, 11 October 1858, Haut Marne; Prefect report, Ain, 20 October 1858; Prefect report, Bourg, 4 November 1858, AN Fic III.

[64] Prefect reports, Aise, 7, 9 January 1859, AN, Fic III.

[65] *Archives Israélites*, April 1859, noted that not one churchman, with the exception of Abbé Delacouture had openly supported the Mortara family.

[66] *Siècle*, 8 March 1861 reprinted the lesson; c.f. *Jewish Chronicle*, (London), 25 March 1865.

[67] Ibid.

[68] *L'Univers*, 15, 16 October 1858.

[69] *Le Constitutionnel*, 18, 20, 22 October 1858.

[70] *Moniteur Universel*, 16 November 1858.

[71] The Drack mentioned in Veuillot's memoirs must refer to David Drach. The name was misspelled in *Oeuvres complètes*. The conversion of David Drach in 1823 was scandalous within the Jewish community because of his family connections. He was born in Alsace in 1791 and trained to become a rabbi. Attracted by the breeze of liberty and modernity, he left the insular environment of Alsace and came to Paris. He worked as the Secretary to the Central Israélite Consistory, and married the daughter of the Grand Rabbi of France. He was then appointed director of the first Jewish school employing the newest pedagogical techniques. At the same time he studied secular subjects, earning a bachelleres-lettres and eagerly sought acceptance by the Christian world of Paris, so much so, that he converted to Catholicism. Following his apostasy he pursued studies in

Catholic theology , and won renown for his editing of the Bible of Vence. He was appointed librarian for the Duc de Bordeaux (son of the Duchesse de Berry). Five years later (1832) he was appointed Librarian of the Congregation of the Propagation of the Faith at Rome. Henceforth, his activities were divided between Rome and Paris. He was especially eager to convert his fellow Jews. c. f. Paul Klein, "Mauvais juif, mauvais chrétien," *Revue de la Pensée juive*, 17 (1951): 87-103; Paul Catrice, *L'harmonie entre l'église et le judaisme*, (doctoral thesis, Faculty of Lille, 1972), 636, 760-61.

[72] Louis Veuillot, *Oeuvres complètes*, IV, *Mélanges*, (Paris: P. Lethielleux, 1925), 316; Eugène Veuillot, *Louis Veuillot*, 9th edition (Paris, 1904), III, 216-222. These articles appeared daily in *L'Univers* from the end of October 1858 through January 1859.

[73] Ibid.

[74] Alexandre Weill, *Lettres fraternelles à Louis Veuillot*, (Paris, 1858).

[75] Aristide Astruc, *Les juifs et Louis Veuillot*, (Paris, 1858); c. f. Arnold Ages, "Veuillot and the Talmud," in *Jewish Quarterly Review*, 64 (January 1974): 229-60.

[76] *L'Univers*, 19 November 1858.

[77] Colmar Consistory to the Central Consistory, November 1858; Nancy Consistory to Central Consistory, 21 November 1858; Strasbourg Consistory to Central Consistory, 25 November 1858; Marseilles Consistory to Central Consistory, 7 December 1858; ACIC, 3E, Affaires politiques.

[78] Central Israélite Consistory to Minister of religion, 20 November 1858, 2 December 1858, AN, F 18, 1587.

[79] Ibid.; Minister of justice to Minister of religion, 29 November 1858, AN, F 18, 1587.

[80] *Times*, (London), 22 November 1858.

[81] Minister of justice to Minister of religion, 24 November 1858, AN, F 19, 11031.

[82] Minister of justice to Minister of religion, 2 December 1858, AN, F 19, 11031; Albert, 162-65.

[83] *Times*, (London), 25 November 1858.

[84] Adolph Crémieux to Central Consistory, Paris, 10 December 1858, ACIC, 3E, Affaires politiques.

[85] Albert, 163; Central Consistory, Paris, 10 December 1858, ACIC, 3E, Affaires politiques.

[86] *Archives Israélites*, February 1859.

[87] *Jewish Chronicle*, (London), 31 December 1859.

[88] *L'Univers*, 18, 19, 26 November 1858.

[89] *Archives Israélites*, November 1858.

[90] *L'Univers Israélite*, November, December 1858.

[91] Andre Chouraqui, *L'Alliance Israélite Universelle et la renaissance juive contemporaine, (1860-1960)*, (Paris: presses universitaires, 1965), 18-23.

[92] Ibid., 25; *L'Archives Israélites*, January, February, 1859; c. f. Posener, Adolph Cremieux, 183.

[93] Chouraqui, 26-27; Posener, *Cremieux*, 183-85; Narcisse Leven, *Cinquante ans d'histoire*, (Paris: Alcan, 1911), I, 69-74.

[94] Ibid.; Zosa Szajkowski, "The Schools of the Alliance Israelite," *Historica Judaica*, 22, (1960): 3-22.

[95] Leven, I, 69-71.

[96] Robert Wistrich, *Revolutionary Jews from Marx to Trotsky*, (London, New York: Barnes and Noble, 1976), 141.

[97] Theodore Zeldin, *France, 1848-1945*, II, 1026.

[98] Volli, 27-28; *Jewish Chronicle*, (London), 30 September, 14 October 1859, translated this article.

[99] Gramont to Walewski, Rome, 30 October 1858, AMAE, CP; c. f. *Daily News*, (London), 24 November 1858; *Jewish Chronicle*, (London), 26 November 1858.

[100] Gene Bernardin, "The Origins and Development of Racial Antisemitism in Fascist Italy," *Journal of Modern History*, 49 (1977): 432; Leon Poliakov, "Antisemitism and Christian Teaching," *Midstream*, 12 (1966): 13-18.

[101] Zeldin, France, II, 1036-37; Dansette, I, 280-81.

[102] *Morning Advertiser*, (London), 30 October 1858; *L'Univers Israélite*, November 1858.

[103] Eugene Veuillot, 224.

[104] Ibid.

[105] Ibid., 223-24.

[106] Prefect of Oise to Minister of religion, Beauvais, 29 October 1858, AN, F19, 2502.

[107] Eugene Veuillot, 224.

[108] *Times*, (London), 20 October 1858; *Jewish Chronicle*, (London), 24 February 1865.

[109] Brown, 250.

[110] Volli, 90-120.

[111] Rémond, 63-66; L. Schwartz and N. Isser, "Some Involuntary Conversion Techniques," *Jewish Social Studies*, 43 (1981): 1-10.

Chapter III

The Roman Question

The Roman Question, which arose in the course of Italian unification, became the single most enduring and bitter political issue during the Second Empire. Italian unification had revealed how fragile the Pope's temporal power was, and how threatening Italian nationalism could become even to the possession of Rome itself. The debates that arose over French foreign policy in Italy became the overriding issue. As threats to the Papal power intensified, Veuillot's attacks became even fiercer and his language more vituperative. The liberal Catholics also joined the fray by attacking the government from the pulpit and by sending protesting circulars to their dioceses.[1] Antisemitism became a part of the impassioned polemics over the organization of the Italian Confederation and the extent of the Pope's temporal power because the bitterness of the debates and the irreconcilable political issues provided a fertile field for the rhetoric of religious prejudice and its accompanying stereotypes. Moreover, as we have seen, Louis Veuillot, who spearheaded the ultramontane antisemitism, saw the Jews as the surrogate symbols of secularism and modernism, the two enemies of the Papacy and the true faith. His editorials also attacked Protestants and Freemasons, whom he regarded as Jewish allies and as equally dangerous adversaries.

Religious freedom and nationalism were twin developments of modernism. Hence, for him, attacks upon Jews and Protestants were, in reality, a part of the arguments which sustained the verities of Catholicism and were intrinsic to the defense of the Papacy. Thus part of his total strategy in defending the temporal power was the inclusion of antisemitism. Veuillot continued by furiously attacking all the Jewish defenses of the Mortaras as evil insults to Christians and their beliefs. He accused the Jewish press, in particular, of defaming Catholics.[2] He further insisted that Jews themselves stole Catholic children, citing as evidence the infamous Drach scandal (a grotesque distortion of the facts).[3] He reiterated the often resurrected blood libel, and fulminated against Jewish clannishness by claiming that only rich proselytes were acceptable to the Jewish community, and that Jews could not assimilate into French life.[4] Jews hastened to refute these calumnies. Although their arguments were impressive, ultramontane vilification continued. Rabbi Klein rebutted Veuillot's arguments in a lengthy theological study. He concluded his work with these words:

> Christian writers have written about us negatively: they will only learn the truth about Judaism when Jews themselves seize the opportunity to defend and explain their faith. Now the time has come for Jews to protest and decry the imputations, impostures, and monstrous calumnies which have emanated from the middle ages and have remained a part of modern Divine Providence. We ask of Him (God) only his justice and that no other than the necessary restraints in the interest of humanity, of confessing publicly that in your polemic against the Jews, you have been guided not by the love of truth but by the ardent desire to obscure it, and that independently of the wrong that you have done to so many men, you battled with God; for the Eternal is the God of truth.[5]

Editorials in the Jewish press sustained and supported such criticism; one editor compared Veuillot to the arch-villain Hamen of Jewish history, because he (Veuillot) exemplified hate of the Jew.[6] Veuillot remained undaunted. In his continuing aggressive articles he found willing allies among the ultramontane papers, especially *Le Monde, Union,* and *Bien Public.* The carefully orchestrated revival of the charge of ritual murder best illustrated the unanimity of the ultramontanes. Boldly restated by Veuillot, this theme was kept on the front pages by the publicity accorded a murder in Roumania.

A child had been murdered in the town of Fokshany on the border of Moldavia-Wallachia. Jews in the town had been unjustly accused of the crime (committed allegedly for religious purposes). In carefully dramatizing the account, the Catholic press reported that a crown of thorns had been placed on the murdered child's brow. *L'Univers* deduced, therefore, that only Jews could have committed such a heinous crime. A Belgian Catholic paper went even further, and declared that the reason Jews had not been punished was because witnesses had been suborned, and that the judges had been bribed.

"Jewish gold has accomplished its task," that paper declared. *L'Univers* not only reproduced this account, but claimed that the information had been obtained from the most reliable of sources. Despite the absence of evidence, that paper continued to maintain that the case was testimony to Jewish hate of Christians.[8] Veuillot was duly supported in these allegations by the other ultramontane papers. Firmly convinced that a Jewish conspiracy caused a miscarriage of justice, Veuillot and friends demanded that the case be investigated by an international commission selected by various consuls. The inquiry was re-opened under the aegis of agents selected by the Great Powers (Great Britain, Austria-Hungary, France, Russia, and Prussia). The results of the investigation proved that Jews were not the murderers of the child. Indeed, they were not even under suspicion. Only two Jews were even mentioned in the case, and they appeared only as witnesses. No crown of thorns had ever been found. Suspicion of murder pointed, instead, to an uncle of the dead child. The Jews were completely exonerated. *L'Univers* finally reproduced some of the story coyly stating: "We did not accuse anyone of murder."[9] Months of vituperative abuse were still accompanied by demands for more evidence. Moreover, the Catholic press, so quick to suspect Jews of murder, remained silent on the final conclusion of the case, and the resultant evidence that had clearly exonerated the Jews.

The antisemitic rhetoric was, in fact, peripheral to the anxieties over the impending Italian war and the fate of the Papacy. It was, however, used as a part of the attack upon "paganism" (another word for secularism) which the conservatives felt was the major factor in the nationalist fervor which threatened the Holy Pontiff. Such was the brochure by Louis Rupert, entitled *L'église et le synagogue*. Louis Rupert was the former secretary of the Archbishop of Metz. He later became an editor of the *Mémorial Catholique* and then *L'Univers* and *Le Monde*. The pamphlet would have little impact without the approbation and publicity given by Louis Veuillot.[10]

The book was a highly inflammatory denunciation of Jews and Judaism. Rupert denied the rights of liberty of conscience and political equality which had been granted to Jews. Such development arose in modern France as a result of the evils of "philosophic indifference." Jews, he claimed, exercised a nefarious influence upon Christian morality throughout history. When Christians attempted to protect themselves, Jews, in turn, accused them of persecution and harassment. These "calumnies of past Christian behavior" stated that the church and kings produced Jewish martyrs, and inflicted barbarous punishments. Indeed, he declared, Jews have erroneously posed as victims of Christian prejudice, and they have been abetted in this misreading of history by such liberals as Robert Peel, Maximo d' Azeglio and Gioberti. Rupert insisted that his main objective was to refute these "audacious recriminations" of the Jews. According to his version of world events, Jews hated all mankind, especially Christians. They were clannish; they practiced secular magic. Rabbinic law commanded Jews to assassinate and steal whenever the opportunity arose. Therefore, the author insisted that the only way Christians could contend with this people was to resort to force. History attested to Jewish perfidies. Throughout the Middle Ages, continued Rupert, Jews were associated with every evil passion, and all the wickedness that afflicted mankind. They aided the Manichean heresy, the invasion of Ghengis Khan, and propagated the materialist philosophy of Averroes and the Albinginsian heresy. They encouraged the struggle between the Papacy and the Empire. Naturally, in the face of such provocations the Western kings took severe and firm action. They suppressed Jewish attacks on the Eucharist, on Christian children, on the cross, and sought to rid society of Jewish crimes (which he claimed still existed in the Damascus Affair of 1840). Rupert concluded his pamphlet: "The kings, in punishing the Jews had good motives, and the Church by its cooperation only did its duty toward its children."[11]

L'Univers Israélite responded to Veuillot's praise of this invective by saying:

> The examples of your literature, books, journals and pamphlets are poor recommendations of your religion. In truth it is better for us to remain victims than to become persecutors. . . . Veuillot has abandoned God. He claims his God is the God of love but he preaches hate and persecution. The pope steals our children and encloses our co-religionists within a ghetto.[12]

Rupert's brochure and its charges were so contrived and irrational that it was hard to believe that it was ever taken seriously. Yet the Jewish press felt constrained to respond to these libels, which were repeated by later antisemitic writers.[13]

Gradually, the French government began to regard L'Univers' frenetic prose with dismay. As Veuillot attacked the government's foreign policy as venomously as he denigrated Jews, the administration became more annoyed, and finally in a response to the protests of the Jewish consistories and in anger at some of his attacks, gave Veuillot an *avertissement*,[14] a deed which afforded the Jewish consistories much satisfaction.[15] What officials had wished to do in December 1858 was finally accomplished three months later, but only *L'Univers* received the warning.[16] The *avertissement* did not end the antisemitism in the debates over the Roman Question. Some Catholics began to identify Jews as the source of Italian problems; this impression, emphasized by French clericals, was reinforced by the statements of Pius IX. During and after the Sardinian French-Austrian war, many riots occurred in Bologna and later, during the summer of 1859, mobs assailed several nunneries in Ferrara. The Pope, in a series of talks, asserted that Jews led these attacks as a part of their revenge upon the church for the seizure of Edgardo Mortara.[17] During the summer, following the successful rebellion in the legations, an ultramontane correspondent duly repeated the charge that the Jews "have risen en masse to revenge the Mortara family! The Jews have done it all."[18] The Paris correspondent of an English Catholic paper also wrote: ". . . The Israelites appear to be the prime movers in all this Italian difficulty, which as I already noticed, has its whole origin in the misunderstanding between France and Austria about the Mortara boy, who is as much the cause of this war as the key of Jerusalem's sepulchre was of the Crimean campaign. . . ."[19]

As the threats to Papal power were intensified by the revolts in the Duchies and the Romagna, and when, through the postponement of the international congress, these territories were annexed by Sardinia Piedmont, the controversy intensified. Henceforth, Catholics, if not in agreement on their vision of the state, were united in their defense of the Pope's temporal power. Veuillot's responses became so bitter, and his invective so outrageous, that when he illegally published the Pope's Encyclical on January 1860, his paper was suppressed, and he was denied authorization to publish another.[20] Veuillot's exit from the daily press did not, however end the antisemitic polemics of the ultramontanes. The campaign of invective directed against Jews and Protestants formed a part of the defense of the Pope's temporal power, because as outsiders, these groups represented the forces of secularism and liberalism. One editor described the sentiment in this vein:

> Europe, more and more degraded, has fallen under the ignoble yoke of the deicidal race. A few Jews decide on the fate of the nations by either tying or loosening the knot of their purse. They, moreover,

direct the revolutionary movements by means of
the journals which they have bought. . . . Their
ancestors caused the saviour of the world to be lift-
ed up to the cross. They now drag to it his vicar,
assisted by scribes, pharisees and firebrands of
Europe. . . ."[21]

Hence, any event that could discredit Jews illustrated, at least for the
ultramontanes, Jewish baleful influences. Such an episode was the Mirès
scandal which occurred in 1861. Jules Mirès was a banker and journalist, a
man consumed with dreams, great enterprises and financial speculation.
Mirès was born in 1809, son of a watchmaker who had migrated from Gen-
eva. He left school at the age of twelve, and his early years were not
distinguished. However, after his arrival in Paris, he achieved prominence.
With the aid of a well-known Jewish businessman, Moïse Millaud, he purchased the newspaper *Journal des chemins de fer* in 1849 and turned it into a
financial journal. Subsequently he founded the *Conseiller du peuple*, and then
in 1850 and 1852 acquired two major Bonapartist papers, *Le Pays* and *Le
Constitutionnel*. His ownership of the latter papers sustained the popular
canard of antisemites: that Jews controlled the press.

During this same period Mirès expanded his entrepreneurship by
founding a bank with Millaud, the Caisse des Actions Réunies, which he
later expanded into an investment bank in partnership with Félix Solar (who
was also Jewish). In 1853 this new bank became the Caisse Générale des
Chemins de Fer. He used his newspapers to promote his various enterprises such as the Credit foncier of Nevers, the rebuilding of the port of
Marseilles, the creation of railroads in Spain and the Papal States, and the
negotiations for a Turkish loan in 1860. As he became enormously wealthy
and powerful he alienated rival bankers, the Pereires and Rothschilds. One
of Mirès investors accused the banker of fraudulent dealings. (Whether the
collaborator was genuinely disgruntled or instigated by rival bankers is
still unknown). Consequently, Mirès was arrested 17 February 1861; in July
of that year he was tried, found guilty, and sentenced to five years in prison. His partner, Solar, was tried and sentenced in absentia.[22] A successful
appeal to the Court of Cassation led to the order for a retrial at Douai in
1862, where Mirès was exonerated and freed.[23] Mirès became the symbol-
ic stereotype of the Jewish banker and flamboyant millionaire. Indeed, he
fired the imagination of several dramatists, notably Alexandre Dumas, fils
(*La Question d'argent*) and François Ponsard (*Monseignor Million, La Bourse*);

and novelist Oscar de la Vallée (*Les manieurs d'argent*). While many of these depictions were sympathetic, the antisemites found that the scandal confirmed their deepest suspicions about Jews. Mirecourt, in his study of eminent Frenchmen, vented his anger in his portrait of Mirès,[24] and the socialist Duchene and Proudhon, too seized the affair to reinforce their hostility of the forces of capitalism and modernity.

The Affair also presented conservatives with an opportunity to score antisemitic coups. In Alsace, an area filled with strong religious antagonisms, a paper edited by a priest attacked the liberal newspaper, *La Presse* (owned by the Jew Solar), and the semi-official jounals *Constitutionnel* and *Pays* (owned by Mirès), which the editor claimed mocked "good Christians and the men of honor."[25] Moreover, the Jewish community noted that there were no Catholic or episcopal church criticisms of such polemics.[26] Even more alarming to the Jewish community was a sharper invective entitled "La Banque noire" which appeared in Paris on 28 October 1861 in *Le Monde*. This article did not directly discuss the Mirès Affair, but rather attacked Jewish money lenders in general, and specifically those in Alsace, in these words:

> Jewish "mercantilism" is almost the only cause of the ruin of a great number of rural enterprises. The Jews have, for a long time, exploited on a vast scale our most beautiful and fertile province (Alsace); they are the ones who have established a type of lending institution . . . which covers the entire countryside from one end to another; an institution I will name "Banques noires," and these function with such subtle perfection that they ruin the farmer. . . . The peasant finds it impossible to escape or avoid the financial nets held by the Jews. They (the Jews) are everywhere. They, alone, have money; they offer it to the peasant; they control all sales, indeed, all transactions. . . . The farmer is honest and credulous; he works hard and does not have time to learn all the swindles that Jews can perpetrate. The Jew eats well, lives well, and is enriched by not working. . . ."[27]

The Jewish consistories rightfully regarded this article with dismay, for Alsace had a long bitter tradition of antisemitic violence. The Colmar consistory requested that the Central consistory insitute action against the paper;[28] the Strasbourg consistory complained to the Ministry of Cults.[29] As in the Mortara Affair, the Central consistory, though angry, was loathe to undertake any retaliatory action, citing the Crémieux and Bethmont advice in the case of Louis Veuillot in 1858.[30] To sue the editors of *Le Monde* for libel, they claimed, would be difficult and fruitless since the law protected the press. The Jewish Consistory in Strasbourg disagreed, insisting that the article produced "direct incitation to hate," and hence, they brought a suit against *Le Monde*.[31] Moreover, the government supported the views of the Alsatian consistories. The Minister of Interior requested the Minister of Justice to prosecute the editor because the former thought that the "words of this article bore the imprint of such malevolence that an *avertissement* would be an insufficient punishment."[32] The provincial libel suit was stopped when the Minister of Justice ordered that the case be tried before the correctional tribunal of Paris. The tribunal handed down its judgement on 29 March 1862; the director of *Le Monde*, Taconet, and the author of "La Banque Noire," Abbé Abrist, were guilty of "exciting citizens to hatred and contempt of each other." They were fined 500 francs.[33]

Clerical antisemitism was the strongest in Alsace; the result of a long history of religious antagonisms and strong conservatism. Although the church was devoted to the Papacy, the clergy, for the most part, exercised restraint, retreating from the "excitement that they had shown at the beginning of the Italian campaign."[34] The Archbishop, Raess, a committed ultramontane, contributed to the clergy's moderation by cautioning the priests to avoid comment on the Encyclical, and enforced his edict by reprimanding those who disobeyed.[35] Moreover, the people themselves were disinterested in the Italian question, and preferred that their priests refrain from political agitation.[36]

Nevertheless, a propaganda campaign to defend Papal interests was undertaken through the mass circulation of pamphlet literature. Some of these brochures used antisemitic rhetoric to make their points. Abbé Poplineau's *Le Pape devant un maire de village* was such a case. The author's argument for the Pope's temporal power asserted that the principles of the French Revolution were being tested in the Italian peninsula. If these new revolutionary principles were firmly ensconced by the triumph of nationalism, the Pope's leadership would be threatened, priests would be physically assaulted, and both private property and marriage would be eradicated. Catholics, therefore, must save themselves by turning back to the leadership of the clergy. The church would protect them against "Jews, Protestants, and Socialists," and would subsequently restore the French legitimate sovereigns.37 Another brochure entitled, *Trois garçons causent avec leur curé sur le Denier de St. Pierre*, was widely distributed in the Eastern provinces. It, too, spoke of a Jewish conspiracy to strip the Pope of his powers.38 The pamphlet *Der Biersipp de Schmiedness und der Papst*, however, caused the most anxiety to the Jewish community. The brochure was simply written in Alsatian patois, and consisted of a dialogue between a "miserable drunkard named Joseph, the beer drinker, and a virtuous bright goldsmith, Francis." Francis met Joseph, by chance, in the brasserie, reading the newspapers about the Papal problem. Joseph could not understand the complex issues, so Francis explained them to him thus: "The subjects of the Pope are happy. The French pay twice the taxes that the Romans do. Piedmont has a much higher crime rate. The English and German Protestants and Russians prefer to live in Rome, because Romans enjoy more liberties. Roman citizens are the happiest in the world. They have the most efficient government because they are ruled by priests." Then Joseph asked, "Why do the Papal subjects revolt?" Francis explained that outsiders tried to impose their ideas and government on the people. He went on:

> The Jews are furious at not having their Messiah, yet they wish to take the Pope away from Catholics. They started the uproar over the Mortara Affair. Many Protestants have wished for the fall of the Pope. Bad Catholics wished to embarrass the Pope because he proclaims God's commandments to the world, and he has forbidden perjury, adultery, and theft. The Piedmontese wish to annex the Papal States; the republicans wish to turn the States into a republic. . . . The children of Israel would wish to sell the wealth of the Church."39

The author of this pamphlet was reputed to be the Curé of Haguenau, Abbé Gerber. Certainly, the church was known to have given it support because for three weeks this pamphlet had been freely distributed throughout the towns and the countryside, and given away to the children in various primary schools. The press either disregarded or actively supported the brochure, which hampered the government's attempt to reduce its importance, for in Alsace the press was either dominated by Catholics or Protestants. The local administration had not been able to establish their own papers, and, therefore, semi-official rebuttals were difficult.40

The Jewish community leaders were rightfully nervous, because they had previously been exposed to riotous behavior and, therefore, they deemed that some action was necessary. They resented the brochure's imputations and protested vigorously what they felt were provocations to violence. The central authorities responded to the consistories by ordering local officials to seize the Gerber pamphlet in 1860. The seizure, however, was not accompanied by law suits or prosecutions for defamation, as was often customary, because the procureurs had learned that the Archbishop himself had carefully edited the proofs of the aforesaid brochure. Moreover, the procureur was informed that the Archbishop supervised all of the local publications on the Roman Question. Although the government policy was consistent in protecting Jewish rights, local officials remained equally consistent in their efforts to avoid an open confrontation with the regional institutional authorities. Therefore, the procureur felt the seizure of the pamphlet was sufficient.[41]   If the ultramontanes had used antisemitism in their campaign to defend the Pope, the government was ready to use Jewish mistreatment as a potent criticism to discredit the Papacy and its clerical supporters. If Pius IX had disappointed the emperor by his recalcitrant denial of the return of Edgardo Mortara, Louis Napoleon found a "silver lining" in his failure. The emperor saw the Mortara Affair as an event that could compromise the Pope in the eyes of Europe and the moderate Catholics. He said: "The more anger that can be aroused against him (the Pope) the easier it will be to force upon him those sacrifices that the reorganization of Italy will impose."[42]

The emperor sought and found new allies among conservative republicans and anti-clericals, especially in the newspapers *Le Siècle, La Presse*, and *L'Opinion Nationale*. Supposedly in opposition to the government, they supported Italian nationalism fervently, and favored the weakening of the Pope's temporal authority. Pamphlets were also published—some of which were inspired by the government.[43] Among some of these writers could be found liberals, conservative republicans, and anticlericals. One of the best known literary figures of this "so-called liberal leaning" was Edmond About.

About was born in Lorraine in 1828 in moderate circumstances. Possessing an independent mind and agile wit, About succeeded brilliantly in school, and received many scholarships. He gained admittance to the prestigious Ecole Normale, where he graduated at the top of his class. Upon his graduation he studied archeology in Greece and consequently published his observations in a book, *La Grece contemporaine* (1855). This book brought him critical acclaim and fame because of his penetrating criticism, his sharp wit, and his elegant prose style. Although he was an avowedly conservative republican, he was also passionately committed to the cause of nationality, and was an ardent anticlerical. Through his literary friends, he gradually came into contact with Achille Fould, Princess Mathilde, and Prince Napoleon (the "so-called liberals" of the Second Empire). The shared sympathy for Italian, German and Roumanian nationality soon led About to cooperate with the government in writing for its newspapers and brochures.[44] After collaborating on several semiofficial brochures, he wrote innumerable articles for the *Opinion Nationale*, a liberal newspaper which supported the empire's foreign policy.[45] His efforts were duly recognized by a grateful government by the award of the Legion of Honor; his literary merit earned him election to the French Academy a year before his death in 1884.[46]

During the year 1858, About had visited Italy and spent considerable time in Rome. An astute and careful observer, he recorded his impressions of the Papacy. These essays came to the notice of government officials who had them published in the official newspaper *Moniteur Universel* in June and July 1858.[47] The series provoked consternation among French clericals and created enormous agitation in the Papal court, because the articles were sharply critical of Roman rule. Protests of the Papal nuncio led the French government (preparing for war) to discontinue the articles.[48] The entire issue seemed dormant. Subsequently, the Mortara Affair occupied the center of public attention from September to November 1858; and About was permitted to defend the young Mortara in another article in the *Moniteur Universel* in a restrained fashion.[49] The controversy over the Mortara Affair was suppressed at the end of November, but Jewish issues were not. The government wanted to prepare public opinion for a coming conflict in Italy and officials were ready to use any weapons available to sustain the cause of Italian nationality.

As the controversy began to grow, stimulated by the press and a semiofficial brochure entitled *L'Empereur Napoléon III et l'Italie* which demanded reforms in Italy, the emperor requested About to expand and revise the earlier articles on the Roman Question. By 10 March 1859, About had almost completed his assignment. The Emperor, Morny, and Fould read the draft and made comments and suggested various editorial changes.[50] The finished manuscript was entitled *La Question romaine*, and published in Brussels (so as not to offend the censors), and appeared in Paris in May 1859 in the midst of the Austrian, Piedmontese, Franco War. After a limited circulation, the pamphlet was seized, but not until after the clericals were angered.[51] Their ire was aroused because About's book went far beyond the earlier articles in its attacks upon the Roman administration. He cited the persecution of Jews as one of the abuses of human rights, revealing the injustices of the canon law and its inhumanity when practiced against Jews. He said:

> The church undertakes to keep Jews alive and miserable. It makes enclosures for them as we do for curious animals in the zoo. . . . They are allowed to circulate throughout the city, to show Christians how dirty and degraded a man is when he is not a Christian, but when night comes, they are put under lock and key. . . . I have learned that the humblest offices in the humblest administrations are inaccessible to the Jews. . . . Manufactures are forbidden to them. . . . The most unfortunate Jews in Italy are the Jews of Rome. The neighborhood of the Vatican is as fatal to them as to Christians. Beyond the Apennines far from the government, you will see them less poor, less oppressed and less bowed down. From the date of this book it is still not a year passed since the little Mortara boy was abducted for the benefit of the House of Catechumens. . . ."[52]

About concluded his acerbic commentary by suggesting that the remedy for Papal misrule was to reduce the size of the Papal States and "at the worst leave Rome to the Pope."[52] About's book was sharply criticized by both the liberal and conservative Catholics, and even evoked brochure rebuttals. The Roman nuncio complained, and the government removed the book from the stores. Nevertheless, the *Roman Question* had achieved Napoleon III's purpose to create discussion.[54]

The theater, too, provided an emotional vehicle by which the Mortara Affair could be subtly interjected into the debates over the Roman Question. The drama *La Tireuse de Cartes* by Victor Séjour was just such a case. Jean Mocquard was co-author, but his name never appeared on the play.

The two dramatists, entirely different in training, birth, and social class, had only their intense loyalty to the emperor in common. It proved to be enough. Victor Séjour, a black man, was born in 1817 in New Orleans, Louisiana. He was educated in private schools, where he received a sound classical education. His parents then sent the young man at age seventeen to Paris because they wished to take advantage of the social mobility available to blacks in France. He remained, pursuing a literary career. The publication of his poem, *Le Rétour de Napoleon*, in 1841, caught the attention of Louis Napoleon and through this meeting Séjour met Jean Mocquard. He then wrote for the theater and became the most prolific dramatist of his time, producing a new play almost every year. Most of his dramas were financially successful until the 1870s when the public tired of them.[55] The critics were more reserved about Séjour's talents.[56] His plays were strongly representative of nineteenth century French romanticism, filled with heroic figures and noble themes. His characters were often pasteboard in their conception; the plots and dialogue frequently appeared contrived and generously filled with hyperbole, and the action over dramatic.

Jean Mocquard, Séjour's sometime collaborator, had a contrasting social position, education and personality. He was born in 1791 in Paris, of well-to-do parents. Having successfully studied law, he entered the diplomatic corps, serving the Emperor Napoleon. In 1812 he was promoted to Secretary of the Legation in Bavaria, but the fall of the First Empire ended his diplomatic career, and he practiced law. After the Revolution of 1830 he was appointed sous-prefect, a position he held until 1839. The next year he met Louis Napoleon, and, already a devoted Bonapartist, turned his energies to the young pretender's cause. Following the Revolution of 1848, Mocquard became the Prince's private secretary, a post he held until his death in 1864. As private secretary to the emperor he was involved in the most personally intimate and important political missions of the government.

Although his fame and reputation rested upon his political accomplishments, he was also a novelist and a playwright. Besides his collaboration on *La Tireuse des cartes*, he wrote two later plays with Séjour. As with Séjour, critics regarded Mocquard as a mediocre writer, despite the variety and quantity of his output.[57]

The peculiar circumstances of the Séjour-Mocquard authorship are still unclear. How much inspiration was provided by the emperor or Prince Napoleon is certainly not known. However, Mocquard's position in the government gave the drama political significance, hence his name was omitted from the title page.

When the play was submitted to the censors, prior to receiving permission for production, the members of the board were unaware of the true nature of the author's political connection. Because the precedent for protecting clerical institutions had been firmly established, the censors reacted in their customary conservative fashion. They were perturbed by the subject matter, and were dubious about permitting the performance. They pointed out that the drama "raised questions which were inspired by the recent baptism of the Mortara child which can be applied to actual international and religious policies."[58] However, rumors reached them of the high esteem the author enjoyed at court, and as specified by law, the censors consulted the Minister of State. He, in turn, responded by firmly insisting that the play must be produced. Confronted with explicit orders from above, the censors nevertheless remained anxious about the controversial nature of the drama. They, therefore, demanded deletions and changes within the play before granting their final authorization. These alterations, they declared, were necessary in order to "attenuate that which would arouse too much religious antagonism, by eliminating all that appears blasphemous or impious."[59] In addition, they insisted that religious figures not be involved in the child's disappearance, and the censors further urged that the plot should instead focus upon the rivalry of the two mothers for possession of the daughter.[60] Pushed by higher authority, the censors reluctantly permitted the production and hoped that their rewriting would prevent controversy.

That, however, was not the government's major goal. Officials did not wish to arouse anger, but they hoped to dampen clerical agitation. Consequently, the news of Mocquard's collaboration was deliberately leaked to the press and to the court. These were, then, the circumstances surrounding the opening of the play on 11 December 1859 at the Porte St. Martin Theater.[61]

The play's central theme was the secret baptism of a Jewish baby girl by a Christian neighbor, who was caring for her. When the Jewish parents claimed their baby, the neighbor secreted her in a convent, to be raised as a Catholic. The woman subsequently died without revealing the child's location to the distraught parents. The Jewish father died and left his wife, Gema, wealthy, but bereft of her child. She disguised herself as a moneylender and fortune teller, and travelled all over the world in a quest for her baby. Finally, years later, Gema (the Jewish mother) discovered that her daughter had been adopted by a noble Catholic family. Gema attempted to retrieve her daughter, who, in turn, was torn between love and duty.[62]

Opening night was exciting, for everyone who was politically knowledgeable was aware of Mocquard's contribution to the play. [63] Further, great care and expense had been lavished upon the scenery; and the acting of the two mothers had been deemed superior.[64] In contrast to other first nights which were replete with the "mothers of actresses, critics, and theatrical celebrities," at this performance the theater was filled with prominent social and political personalities, because "the Emperor and the empress came to applaud Mocquard and remained until the end, gracing the performance with importance."[65]

An even greater spur was the controversy it aroused in the press. *Le Monde, Gazette de France*, and *L'Ami de la Religion* disliked the play and accused the author of being a bad Catholic. Séjour defended his drama by claiming that he was only defending family rights. *Le Siècle* pointedly emphasized that the imperial couple gave the signal for applause, that the empress was very moved by the drama, and that the audience was enthusiastic with their clapping and hurrahs.[66] Indeed, the play was a smash hit in Paris, despite the attacks by the clericals, for as one British observer noted:

> Who could fail to discover excellence in a dramatic
> production written by an official high in imperial
> favor ? . . . The success obtained by M. Mocquard
> and Séjour . . . would certainly not have attracted
> any unusual attention but for the peculiar circum-
> stances by which it has been surrounded."[67]

The censors in the provinces were just as worried about reaction to the play as those in Paris. Their queries, however, were handled differently. Local officials were given discretionary power on whether to produce the play in their arrondissements. Those prefects who feared adverse reaction banned performances. Others gave their assent. The play was successful in some areas, as in Strasbourg, where Jews and Protestants attended in force.[68] In clerical areas, attendance was poor.

Thus the Roman question, which erupted with such passion in 1860-61 continued until 1871. It became the divisive issue that corroded French political life. It sundered the precarious alliance between the government and the church. Yet the debates, which were trivial, prejudiced, and irreconcilable, seemed to have little impact upon the average Frenchmen.[69] Nevertheless, the arguments reopened basic conflicts, not only in church-state relationships, but also in the perceptions of the nature of French society which had divided French political life in 1848. It was in the debates ostensibly over the fate of the Papacy that these differences were revealed, for the ultramontane Catholics resented the forces of nationalism, religious freedom and individual rights. They supported tradition, authority, and the institutions that preserved morality and stability. The Jews became involved in these debates only as surrogate symbols of the beliefs of each side. The administration used Jewish persecution as an example of the evil of the Papal regime and actively defended religious liberty. The Jews, therefore, had no alternative but to support the government and Italian nationalism. Jewish communal and ethnic interests forced them to identify with the activities of the liberals and anticlericals. Thus the ultramontane perceptions of Jewish enmity of the Papacy were reinforced by the government's arguments and the Jewish press.

As the struggle continued and crises kept recurring in the Italian quest for unification, the government persisted in its support of nationality and modernism. Even though the church was regarded as an indispensable and important agency of stability, the government could not allow it to break French laws or impede important state policy, nor could the government condone what it considered the zealous, reactionary, fanatic religiosity expressed by the ultramontanes.

1 Lynn M. Case. *French Public Opinion on War and Diplomacy during the Second Empire,* (Philadelphia: Univ. of Penn. Press, 1954), 109-150; Natalie Isser, *The Second Empire and the Press,* (Hague, Nijhoff, 1974), 97-150.

2 *L'Univers,* 12 January 1859.

3 *L'Univers,* 10, 12 January 1859; The wife of Drach (a Jewish convert to Catholicism), refused to abandon Judaism and left him, taking the children with her. Drach won custody of the children in the courts. He baptized them and raised them as Catholics. Klein, "Mauvais juif," *Revue de la Pensée juive,* 83-87; Catrice, 240-48.

4 *L'Univers,* 1, 2, 3 January 1859.

5 S. Klein, *Judaism ou la vérité sur le Talmud,* (Paris, 1859).

6 *L'Univers Israélite,* March 1859, July 1859.

7 *Journal des Débats,* 10 March 1859.

8 *L'Univers,* 10 March 1859.

9 *L'Univers,* 12 March 1859; *L'Univers Israélite,* March 1859; *Archives Israélites,* April 1859; *Jewish Chronicle,* (London), 18 March 1859.

10 *L'Univers,* 12 March 1859; c. f. Jacob Katz, *From Prejudice to Destruction,* (Cambridge, Mass.: Harvard Univ. Press, 1980), 140-41; Catrice, 566.

11 Louis Rupert, *L'église et le synagogue,* (Paris, 1859).

12 *L'Univers Israélite,* September 1859.

13 Ibid., Gougenot des Mousseaux cited Rupert in his book *Le juif, le judaisme, et la judaisation des peuples chrétiens,* (Paris, 1869). The second edition was reprinted with Drumont's help. See pp. 117-19.

14 *Avertissement*, AN, F 18, 423.

15 Strasbourg Jewish Consistory to Central Jewish Consistory, 3E, Affaires Politiques, ACCI.

16 Minister of Religion to Minister of Interior, Paris 1859, AN, F 18, 423.

17 *Times*, (London), 22 April 1859.

18 Ibid.

19 *Times*, (London), 22 April 1859.

20 Dossier on *L'Univers*, AN, F, 18, 423. After the suppression of his paper, Veuillot visited Rome where he was offered shares in a Roman railway owned by M. Mirès, the Jewish banker and speculator. The editor of the London *Jewish Chronicle* thought perhaps the banker was only the instrument in the case. *Daily Telegraph*, 22 February 1860.

21 *Gazette de France*, translated in Jewish *Chronicle*, (London), 18 October 1861.

22 William E. Echard, *Historical Dictionary of the French Second Empire 1852-1870*, (Westport, Conn.: Greenwood Press, 1986), 405-07; Louis Girard, *La politique des travaux publics du Second Empire*, (Paris: Colin, 1952), 268-75; Jules Mirès, *A mes juges, ma vie et mes affaires*, (Paris, 1961).

23 *Jewish Chronicle*, (London), 29 November 1861.

24 Eugene de Mirècourt, *Mirès, Galerie des contemporains*, (Paris, 1869).

25 *Jewish Chronicle*, (London), 29 November 1861.

26 Ibid.

27 *Le Monde*, 28 October 1861.

28 Strasbourg Consistory to Central Israelite Consistory, 13 November 1861, AN, F 19, 11031; Albert, 164.

29 Strasbourg Consistory to Minister of Religion, 14 November 1861, AN, F 19, 11031.

30 Albert, 164-65.

31 *Jewish Chronicle*, (London), 17 January 1862; 25 April 1862.

32 Minister of Interior to Minister of Justice, 14 November 1861, An, F 19, 11031.

33 AN, F 18, 302; Claude Bellanger, Jacques Godecourt, Pierre Guiral, and Fernand Terrou, *Histoire generale de la presse française*, (Paris: Presses Universitaires, 1969), II, 316; *Jewish Chronicle*, (London), 25 April 1862.

34 AN, F18, 302.

35 Procureur Report, 23 February 1860, AN, BB30, 450.

36 Maurain, 386.

37 Procureur Reports, Colmar, 10 July 1860, AN, BB30, 376.

38 Austin Gough, " Bishop Pie's Campaign against the Nineteenth Century," in Theodore Zeldin (ed.), *Conflicts in French Society*, (London: Ungar and Allen, 1970), 155-56.

39 Ibid.

40 Edmond About, *Lettres d'un bon jeune homme à sa cousine Madeleine*, (Paris: 1861); F. Rapp, *Histoire des dioceses de France*, (Paris: Beauchesne, 1982), 234; Procureur Reports,

Colmar, Strasbourg, 19, 21 February 1860, AN, BB30, 450.

41 Maurain, 387; Procureur Reports, An BB30, 376; AN, BB30, 450.

42 Cavour to Villamarina, Turin, 25 November 1858. *Carteggio Cavour Nigra dal 1858 al 1861*, (Bologna, 1929), I, 213.

43 Isser, *Second Empire and the Press*, 86-87, 157-62.

44 Ibid.

45 These articles were later published in a book entitled *Lettres d'un jeune homme à sa cousine Madeleine*, (Paris, 1862).

46 Marcel Thiébaut, *Edmond About*, (Paris: Galliard, 1936, 7th edition), is the standard biography; "Le centenaire d'Edmond About," *Nouvelle Revue*, 93 (1928): 3-12, 123-31.

47 Isser, *Press and the Second Empire*, 86-87.

48 Ibid.

49 *Moniteur Universel*, 20 October 1858; *Morning Advertiser*, (London), 22 October 1858.

50 Jules and Edmond de Goncourt, *Journal*, (Paris, 1910-1911), I, 214-15.

51 About, *Lettres d'un bon jeune homme . . .*, 242; Isser, *Second Empire and the Press*, 89-90.

52 Edmond About, *La Question romaine*, (Brussels, 1859), 197-200.

53 Ibid.

54 Isser, *The Second Empire and the Press*, 89-90.

55 Rudolphe L. Desdunes, *Nos hommes et notre histoire*, (Montreal: Arbour and Dupont, 1911), 38-42; Edward L. Tinker, *Les ecrits de langue française en Louisiane au XIXᵉ siècle*, (reprint: Wendln Kraus, 1970), 427-31; T. A. Daly, "Victor Séjour," *Phylon*, 4 (1913): 5-16.

56 *L'année littéraire et dramatique*, 2 (1860): 233-34.

57 Ibid.; Echard, *Dictionary*, 408-09.

58 Commission d'Examen, 25 November 1859, AN, F 21, 975; *La censure sous Napoleon III*, (Paris, 1892), 148-49.

59 Ibid.

60 Ibid.

61 Goncourt, I, 321-33; Castelli to Minghetti, Turin, 31 December 1859, *Carteggio Castelli*, (Turin,1890-91), I, 279-80; Vimercati to Castelli, 28 December 1859, Ibid., 276-77; A. Zazi, *La politica estera de Regno delle Due Sicilie*, (1940), 193.

62 Victor Séjour, *La Tireuse des cartes* (Paris, 1859).

63 Maurain, 386; Sacconi to Antonelli, Paris, 25 December 1859, Renato Mori (ed.), *La Questione Romano*, 1861-65, II, 324-35; *Le Constitutionnel*, 28 December 1859.

64 Goncourt, I, 231-32.

65 Ibid.

66 *Archives Israélites*, January, February 1860.

67 Charles E. O'Neill, "Theatrical Censorship in France, 1844-1875," *Harvard Library Bulletin*, 26 (1978): 430-32.

68 Procureur Reports, AN, BB30, 376.

Chapter IV

Clerical Scandals and Politics

Partly in response to the ultramontanes' challenge for a Catholic monopoly, and as a part of the ongoing debate over the Pope's temporal power and its own ideological commitment, the government began to liberalize its institutions. After 1860 there were fewer restrictions on the press, legislative debates were published, and the state began to challenge the Church's role in education. Having already been subjected to bitter polemics, sermons, and brochures attacking the Emperor's Roman policy, the government felt further threatened by the political and propagandizing activity of some of the religious orders, particularly Saint Vincent de Paul. As one court observer commented: "There is a real danger in this clerical association which already has great influence."[1] Circulars appeared, stating official policy which inhibited the growth, activity, and development of many religious orders including the suppression of St. Vincent de Paul.

To bolster its gallican policies and reduce protest, the government permitted, for the first time, the publication of clerical scandals which prior to 1861 had been kept from public scrutiny. Case after case of fraud, child abuse, and immorality (including pederasty) filled newspaper columns, titillating their readers. "Between 1861 and 1863," one historian noted, "the percentage of public school teachers found guilty of criminal offenses was six times higher among members of congregations than among laymen."[2] Unfortunately, two such scandals involved cases of proselytization of Jewish adolescents, which, in turn, exacerbated bad feelings among many Catholics, and offended the Jewish community. Christian proselytization was widespread and very active in the nineteenth century. During the Restoration the Catholic church developed a strong missionary force, not only to convert pagans in underdeveloped areas of the world, but also, to reassert the teachings of the church. Missions were sent throughout the countryside. They usually consisted of six, eight, or ten preachers who worked in a specific region or city. They were well organized, and heavily

financed. The evangelical priests were chosen for their dramatic and ora-
torical flair in preaching, and they further embellished their cause by the
use of rite, ceremonials, processions and chanting. Usually, they enjoyed
the support of the church hierarchy and many government officials. Their
purpose was to teach Catholic ideals, to encourage religious participation
and to denounce the evils of the revolution of 1789. After the revolution of 1830 the Orleanist government stifled the missions. However,
evangelical activity remained widespread and active. Its purpose was to
bring a religious message to those whose spirit had become "anti-Christian."[3]

> There was, moreover, a renewed interest
> in the cult of Mary and an expansion of devotions
> in her honor. In 1836, a mystical priest, Desgenettes,
> of the Paris parish of Notre Dame des Victoires
> dedicated his church to the Immaculate Heart of
> Mary, and there founded a confraternity in her
> honor which attracted a large membership be-
> tween 1840 and 1860. Two members, Theodore and
> Alphonse Ratisbonne were famous missionaries,
> the former was active in both scandals.[4]

Theodore Ratisbonne, the scion of a wealthy assimilated Jewish
Alsatian family, had abjured his heritage, and had become driven by the
ambition to convert his co-religionists to his new faith. His family, scandalized and furious, subsequently disowned him. His brother Alphonse, however, experienced a "miracle" (a vision of the Virgin Mary)[5] and joined him
in his profession of the newly discovered faith. The Ratisbonne brothers
became celebrated for their piety and zeal. Abbé Theodore Ratisbonne,
ardent in the propagation of his adopted religion, founded a new order to
help in his work: the Congregation Notre Dame de Sion, whose declared
mission was to educate young converts and poor Jewish children in the
Christian faith.[6]

Evangelical activities by Protestant ministers also aroused antagonisms, and intensified the emotional atmosphere of religious fervor. The
Jewish community resented and deplored the constant attempts to convert
them, for proselytism threatened the Jewish family and soul.[7] The destruction of the Catholic missions meant that the message had to be delivered
elsewhere, and it was in the schools, the hospitals, and the prisons that the
Catholic missionaries were the most effective. Jews protested vigorously—

sometimes to no avail. An elderly man, Dr. Terquem, was baptized in a hospital as he lay dying, despite strong family objections. In his case the protests of the consistory were denied by the Archbishop of Paris, and was also ignored by the government.[8] Another instance concerned a young soldier, Gerson Braun, who was baptized just before his death.[9] There were also frequent protests over the baptism of children of prisoners, and over the baptism of a runaway by the local curé.[10] In some instances, the Jewish consistories did not always receive the desired support from the local officials or mayors.[11] However, if minors were cajoled into baptism without parental permission, the government always defended family rights against the church. Such was the case of proselytization which came to the attention of authorities in 1861, at the trial of Abbé Mallet, a canon in the Cathedral of Cambrai, which took place in the city of Douai (Nord).

The priest, fifty-four years of age, short and stocky, with a gentle "yet vulgar appearance," dressed in ecclesiastical garb,[12] was accused of kidnapping three minor Jewish girls, as well as seducing two of them. He denied the charges, claiming that his was an act of proselytism. The episode's origins occurred in 1833 when Jacob Bluth's daughter Anna, a teacher, went to Paris seeking a position. Jacob was married to Sarah Levy and had eight children (Anna, Minchen, Adolph, Louise, Louis, Sophie, Isadore and Elisabeth). His oldest child, Anna (born in 1825), met Abbé Ratisbonne, who converted her to Christianity, and at her baptismal renamed her Maria Siona. He was a critical figure not only in her conversion, but was also instrumental in the affairs of the entire family. Through Maria Siona's influence, Abbé Ratisbonne then sought to bring the entire Bluth family into the Catholic Church. Maria Siona sent for her sister, Minchen, who was converted at the age of seventeen and given the name of Gabrielle. The next was father Bluth who came to Paris to visit his daughters and through Maria Siona's arrangements, stayed with Abbé Ratisbonne. The priest was certainly eloquent—within eight days Jacob had been baptized, had taken communion, and was confirmed. (Later Father Theodore admitted to authorities that the conversion of Jacob Bluth lacked both conviction and enthusiasm).[13] Once he accepted the new religion, Jacob Bluth could no longer remain a Hebrew teacher, a position he had enjoyed in his native Weimar and in Prussia. He lived in Paris, giving private German lessons and sent for three other daughters, Louise, Sophie, and Elisabeth, who were subsequently baptised. Maria Siona found a teaching position in Cambrai, and while there she became acquainted with Abbé Mallet, the Canon of the Cathedral. At the end of the year 1853, Abbé Mallet convinced Maria Siona to send for her brother Adolph, who was placed under the supervision of Monseigneur Bonse, the Superior of the Apostolic Missions of Cambrai. Three months later he, too, was converted.

The mother of the family, Sarah Bluth, however, remained committed to Judaism and was determined to prevent the completion of the conversion of the younger children: Isadore, Louise, Sophie, and Elisabeth. She left Paris with the children, and went to London where she sought refuge with wealthy Jewish families. They promised to educate Elisabeth and assure her future. Mrs. Bluth, after consulting the Chief Rabbi of London, agreed to this scheme, providing her rights as a mother were respected. Elisabeth had been baptised in Paris despite her mother's resistance, and the rest of the family was determined to bring her back to France. Meanwhile, the son Adolph had become a professor of English and German in an ecclesiastical college at Douai. Abbé Mallet, with money given him by Msgr. Bonse, purchased a haberdashery (notions) shop for Gabrielle (Minchen). Nurtured and provided for by these churchmen, the children then were able to convince their father to seek his entire family and assert his patriarchal rights.

The father, Jacob, weak both in health and character, authorized Adolph to seek his sister Elisabeth and reunite the family. Adolph succeeded, and the entire Bluth family were soon residing at Cambrai. The three younger daughters, Louise, Sophie, and Elisabeth were sent to Paris to be educated in the school of the Convent of Notre Dame de Sion.

Later that year Louise was sent home from school because of illness. At Cambrai, Mallet convinced the child that she should not remain under the baleful influence of her Jewish mother, but rather with her sister Maria Siona. While at Abbé Mallet's home, it became apparent that Maria Siona had become Abbé Mallet's mistress. Furthermore, both Gabrielle and Louise complained that Abbé Mallet's behavior toward them was much too bold and licentious. The Bluth parents were distressed; they returned to Paris and their son Adolph followed. Both father and son abjured their conversion and embraced Judaism again. At this point, the parents requested that their children be returned home from their Catholic schools. Isadore and his brother Louis were sent home from their school without incident.[14] The problem for Jacob and Sarah Bluth, then, was to locate their daughters—Louise, Sophie, and Elisabeth—who in three different ways disappeared, deliberately secreted from their family by various religious authorities.[15]

Louise was sent home, but she stayed only three days and then disappeared under the pretext of attending mass. Abbé Ratisbonne claimed that he fulfilled the parents' request. The Abbé had claimed that he had told Louise to complain to the Prefect of Paris if her family prevented her from attending mass. However, Louise's later pre-trial testimony and a letter from the Abbé contradicted his story. Abbé Ratisbonne was determined to prevent the loss of Louise's faith portended by her stay with her family, and if necessary, do anything to prevent that eventuality. Although Abbé Mallet was convicted of the actual kidnapping, the police were convinced that the Abbé Ratisbonne had taken an "active and important role" in the abduction of the young girl.[16] Louise, having been warned of her impending spiritual doom, clutched her francs, and three days later took a carriage to the home of Dame Dusaillant, and that lady sent her on to another house. Twenty-four hours later, Abbé Mallet, disguised under a dark cloak and wearing a wig to hide his tonsure, took her to the railroad station and thence to Cambrai, where he hid her in his house.

For two and a half years, Louise was hidden under false names in the convents of the Sainte-Union Order in Belgium and France so that her parents could not find her. Finally, when she came of age she resisted the exhortations to become a nun and returned home.[17] Elisabeth Bluth, too was secreted by her sister, Maria Siona, with the help of several ecclesiastics, including the Mother Superior of the Convent of Sainte-Union and its Vicar-General. She was transported, under many false names, from one convent to another (five or six in all) of the Sainte-Union congregations in France and Belgium.[18] The Abbé Ratisbonne, to further confuse the Bluth parents, while on a trip to Jerusalem mailed a letter from Alexandria, signed by Elisabeth, which stated that she was visiting the Holy Land.[19] Instead she was hidden and transported by Abbé Mallet. The consequences of these unusual conditions, and extreme indoctrination of her captors, upon the young girl was incidence of extreme hallucinations and religious exaltations. She became so deranged that the Mother Superior of the Mother House at Douai petitioned the prefect to permit Elisabeth (now in her mid-teens), to be admitted to a mental hospital in Lille. The government notified her family, but the child was hopelessly insane.[20] To make the situation even more tragic, Maria Siona also became deranged. Rumors abounded that she had become pregnant (as the Canon's mistress), and had had an abortion. This traumatic experience had apparently alienated her from reality. No real evidence, however, was produced at the trial to support such a tale. That did not prevent the spread of the story, and the more anticlerical the journalist, the more eager he was to spread the rumor.[21]

The third sister, Sophie, also kidnapped and hidden in various convents, disappeared completely. The government undertook a long hard search and finally located her after the trial of Canon Mallet. She was found in a convent of the Sisters of Sainte-Union, located near London. She refused to return to her parents despite the efforts of the French government. Her hair had been cut, in preparations for her final vows to become a nun. She avoided her family and scorned her mother.[22]

The Canon, Abbé Mallet, was sentenced to six years hard labor for his role in the kidnapping of these young girls. Though other important churchmen had cooperated, Abbé Ratisbonne felt disgraced by his appearance at the trial, and was constrained to respond to the charges of his involvement.[23] He, of course, denied all charges and indignantly insisted that the Sisters of Notre Dame de Sion did not really attempt to proselytize Jewish youngsters. He blamed the "violent articles of certain newspapers" and "maneuvers of Jews and the impious" for the calumnies and false accusations.[24] The Mother Superior of the Sisters of Sainte-Union, the Vicar General, the Apostolic Missionary of Cambrai, and the other churchmen could not be openly punished without creating new political cleavages and divisiveness, and it is in this arena that the case played a significant political role. For the government could not allow the church to break French laws or impede important state policy, nor could the government condone what it considered the zealous, reactionary, fanatic religiosity expressed by the ultramontanes.

It was, therefore, most fortuitous from the administrative point of view that the Mallet trial opened at Douai in March 1861, because on 14 February La Gueronnière's pamphlet *La France, Rome, et L'Italie,* a government inspired publication, aroused the ire of the more conservative Catholics, the most notable and vociferous of which was Cardinal Pie. The Legitimists and clericals were actively agitating over the Roman question. The affair presented another opportunity for the government to discredit the ultramontanes. *Le Constitutionnel,* a semiofficial newspaper, discussed the trial and gave it coverage, but its language and tone remained circumspectly temperate.[25]

Le Siècle and *L'Opinion Nationale* in Paris covered both the trial of Abbé Mallet and the events surrounding it in miniscule detail, and *l'Opinion Nationale* even reprinted the entire transcript of the judicial proceedings. Both papers' editorials excoriated the Church as a cruel and powerful corporation, which required much firmer supervision and surveillance. *L'Opinion Nationale* compared the religious orders to "termites who bore under the earth to undermine existing structures. . . . It remains evident that they can, under spurious claims, seize our children, make them disappear, laugh at our search and at the cries of the papas and tears of the mothers, and make a mockery of justice in this country." That paper candidly admitted that it gave the affair enormous publicity because it wished to arouse public opinion. Its editor further averred that it was sad that the crime could occur in France, honed by the ideals of 1789. "Under the First Empire our armies destroyed the inquisition in Spain; will the Second Empire permit its reimposition in the country now?"[26]

The *Siècle* noted that the expose of the misdeeds which occurred at Cambrai aroused public indignation. The editor continued: "The church through its clergy and religious congregations has become involved in a sordid affair and abuses the rights of many people. Is religious proselytism useful, desirable, or is it dangerous? . . . Are religious establishments in a position to prevent the investigations of justice and does it not call for the urgent intervention of the civil power?" The case, continued the paper, had offended liberty of conscience, and outraged our moral sense. All of these misdeeds were performed under the aegis of the Church. "Thus understood, thus practiced, religious proselytism is a revolting and immoral action that brings despair to families. . . . We demand in the interest of the sacred principle of the family, that every corporation or association not authorized be dissolved and that the administration exercise surveillance on every clerical establishment."[27]

To further publicize the case, a pamphlet of thirty pages entitled *The Affair of Canon Mallet. A record of the Kidnapping of Minors,* which reproduced the record of the trial, was widely circulated throughout France. It seemed more weighty, because it was widely noted that the brochure did not carry the government stamp to which all other publications were subject. The official origins of the brochure became apparent to everyone when it circulated minus the usual government stamp.[28]

The vehemence of the attack by the opposition alarmed the clericals. Embarrassed by the case, it had seemed prudent for the Catholic papers to avoid the issue. Indeed, *Le Monde* was preoccupied with the Roman question. But they could not completely ignore the strident attacks of their anticlerical enemies. *La Gazette de France* did not attempt to apologize for or exonerate Mallet, but rather deplored the fact that the case presented an opportunity for the anticlericals to attack the Church as a result of the sins of Abbé Mallet.[29] *L'Union* complained that newspapers such as *Constitutionnel, Siècle,* and the *Presse* had used the scandal to attempt to discredit the Papacy, and *L'Opinion Nationale* had been almost gleeful in its exhibition of the sins of the accused. "It is evident that the flaunting of these scandals is not to be a lesson of virtue for the people, but it is a lesson, not against unworthy priests but against all priests, to bring hate against all sacerdotal institutions."[30] The *Journal des Villes et des Campagnes* complained that the debates were heated over the Mallet case and that many of the papers distorted the facts—especially about Abbé Ratisbonne.[31] The Catholic historian, La Gorce, echoed some of these sentiments. Although more liberal than the writers in *Le Monde* and *L'Union*, La Gorce felt that the government's tone contained a certain sharpness over these incidents, and it appeared to desire to punish all the clergy and religious houses for the crimes of one order and the imprudence of a few clergymen."[32] The supremacy of the modern state's sovereignity had to be reaffirmed over the spiritual claims of the Church. The family and its structure were a significant part of the Napoleonic Code, as well as a part of the legitimate concern of the priesthood. Thus the state needed to assert its authority, which in these cases, as in the issue of the Italian policy, was opposed to the clerical one.

Rouland, speaking as a senator in May 1860, had declared that the Emperor and the government officials were sincerely religious, but "the state had the unquestionable right of authority and surveillance over the associations (religious orders).[33] As minister of education and religion, Rouland advised the Emperor to be firm in handling the issues raised by the Mallet Affair. The evidence, he pointed out, was incontrovertible that the Mother Superior and the Congregation of Sainte-Union were responsible for the kidnapping of the Bluth girls and therefore, did not deserve special consideration from the government. Indeed, he asserted, the whole Congregation should be suppressed as punishment for its role in the scandal. The Mother Superior's excuse for her behavior was religious zeal, the need to protect these girls from their Jewish parents—and one of them had become mad from excessive indoctrination. "It would be impossible for the government to admit the legitimacy of such a claim in a country whose laws guarantee the sacred right of the family to raise their children, and assures protection of the principle of liberty for all recognized religions." Further he pointed out that there were irregularities in the forms for the authorization of the Mother-House in Douai when it received its authorization in 1850.[34] The local Prefect, the Council of State, and the Emperor agreed, but the final decision was more moderate. Only the Mother-House at Douai would be closed rather than the whole congregation,[35] primarily because of the supplications of the Archbishop of Cambrai.[36]

The Archbishop of Cambrai had been sympathetic to the actions of Sainte-Union and had reputedly in the past supported similar behaviors in his diocese.[37] The Archbishop and the congregation had been associated with the ultramontanes, and the government was strongly convinced that its case was unassailable. It was defending the law, defending religious freedom, and preventing the excesses of "blind proselytism." However, this also became part of a larger policy which attempted to restrict the congregations, especially those that had large educational roles and those religious bodies most stridently supportive of the Pope, as illustrated by the later suppression of the Order of Saint Vincent de Paul. However, such decisions sharpened and widened the areas of conflict between the clericals and the government.

As the authorities began to move against the Mother-House at Douai, the Archbishop of Cambrai solicited Rouland not to punish the Convent of Douai. The Convent's authorization was not irregular; to suppress the Mother-House would cut off the head and impair the effectiveness of the entire congregation. He continued that for years the sisters had played an important role in the diocese of Cambrai, supervising their own schools and even teaching in community primary classes. Their teaching was highly recommended and respected. "If these excellent teachers have become involved in that unfortunate Bluth affair, it was because Maria Siona, the Catholic part of the family, was regarded as representing the father and his interests." Further he claimed, public opinion supported the nuns and "the confidence of families has not been the least diminished by this unhappy incident."[38] The Municipal Council of Douai agreed unanimously to support the Sisters of Sainte-Union and even sought the help of the mayor of the city to plead their case. Although they repeated some of the same defenses as the Archbishop, they emphasized the economic consequences of the closing of the Mother-House in Douai. The Sisters taught three hundred fifty children from three hundred families. If the Mother-House was closed, "it would put the congregation in jeopardy because of the perturbation of its administration." The three hundred families of Douai would look elsewhere for the instruction of their daughters. "The commerce of the city would be deprived of the spending provided each day by the sisters and their school and by the parents who come to visit their children. This business is in excess of several hundreds of thousands francs."[39]   Neither the local officials nor the Minister of Religion, the Council of State, nor the Emperor himself were moved by these arguments, and the orders for suppression were given. The decree was duly published in the official paper *Le Moniteur Universel*, and the semi-official *Le Constitutionnel*.[40]

The Archbishop was angry. He renewed his correspondence with Rouland. He reiterated the fact that the Sisters of Sainte-Union were not guilty of kidnapping the Bluth girls. That indeed, both girls were afraid of their father—Louise feared for her security and Elisabeth had been "sold" to a London Jewish family. Thus the nuns were justified in their actions! He repeated old arguments, and denied many facts revealed in the trial. Further, he claimed if the Vicar General and Apostolic Missionary Bonse were imprudent, why blame and punish the sisters? Public opinion had and would continue to support the Congregation. No one in the Nord was interested in the Bluth Affair. "My diocese has already been harshly treated this past year. The clergy of France have been astonished by the extreme severity of treatment and the unhappy impression has hardly been calming to the priests and to the faithful. The government, I am sure, would not wish . . . to add to our sadness. You will gain more by being indulgent, . . . which will compromise no one, than by an act of severity . . . of which the public will neither understand its justice nor its necessity."[41]

Having failed to stop the closing of the Mother-House, the Archbishop turned to the media to plead his case. He hoped to arouse public opinion and through an appeal to the Senate, have the decree rescinded.[42] He issued a Circular letter to the clergy of the diocese, containing both his arguments against the government action and the correspondence of the Archbishop and the Minister of religion. The Circular ended with the following words: "What gave the Second Empire its immense popularity and which was so welcomed was its program so clearly and so energetically proclaimed. . . . It is time for the good to be reassured and for the wicked to tremble!"[43]   Then he gave the Circular to the local Catholic press which published it.[44] The government reacted swiftly: regarding the mandements as "absurd,"[45] officials sought to keep the situation defused by manipulating the press which was friendly to the regime. The editor of the *Mémorial de Lille*, Destigny, was given documents and commissioned to respond to the Circular. His subsequent articles were then inserted in the various newspapers of the *arrondissement*.[46] Though Destigny, unlike the editors of opposition press who were more anticlerical, was dispassionate and moderate in his language, he wrote long and penetrating arguments that upset the Catholics. He said that the Circular-letter of the Archbishop which purported to expose all the facts was very biased and one-sided. It did not explain why the Bluth girls were transported to Belgium under false names. The prelate offered no new facts or proofs to warrant any change in the wise decision of the government.[47]

The Archbishop lashed back in a letter to the *Mémorial de Lille*, claiming that the Municipal Council of Douai had unanimously voted to support the Sisters, citing the members' integrity, dignity, and wisdom. In response Destigny asked, did not the members of the Council of State enjoy equal integrity, dignity, and wisdom? [47] The war of words kept the whole scandal before the public eye, so much so that one paper complained that the affair should have long been buried, that the current verbal battles were nothing more than a rehash of the same facts which would convince neither side. "Those who do not want to know will learn what they wish to know. There are always the same beliefs in regard to Sainte-Union, the same attempts to believe that there were 'errors' and too severe a punishment by lay authorities." There were also economic interests involved on the part of the diocese and businessmen to maintain the schools.[48]

The revival of the Affair even caught the attention of the ultramontane press in Paris, where *Le Monde* characterized an "inspired" article of the *Mémorial* as "odious" and reprinted the comments of the Catholic *Propagateur*. Other Catholic papers also reprinted the same comments.[49] The Archbishop's stormy attempts to arouse public opinion had caused widespread press comment especially among the conservatives, and his protests had even reached Paris. But his angry words had not been able to convince the government to remit its policy toward the Sisters of Sainte-Union. Frustrated, the Archbishop issued a second Circular to the priests of his diocese which he both printed as a brochure and publicized in the press.[50]

Once again the officials sent Destigny several dossiers of documents, and he was commissioned to respond.[51] The Archbishop had claimed in his second Circular that the government's charges of irregularities in the records of the Sisters was mistaken and misunderstood. There was no real justification for the severity of punishment in repressing the Mother-House. The *Mémorial* answered, "Monseigneur knows the facts imperfectly. . . . If he would have consulted the archives of his bishopric he would have known that the Sisters participated in the kidnapping of the little girls, and have perpetrated frauds in order to convince the government to grant the authorization that they were not able to obtain with truth and frankness."[52] Again the same arguments were repeated but neither side was able to concede any points. Long into January the debates continued in the press with the government granting documentary assistance to its journalistic friends. The arguments were exacerbated by an open letter of the Bishop of Arras to the Minister of religion supporting the Church's position. The furor was to no avail.[53]

The press struggle, however, had little effect upon public opinion. The government had calculated correctly, that although the public was devout enough, economic and political problems were far more important than the fate of a congregation involved in an imprudent case. Indeed, both conservatives and liberals of the articulate bourgeoisie supported the views of the Minister of religion and education on the dangers of excessive proselytism which violated the civil laws. They were, however, irritated by the comments and articles of the opposition newspapers which were so rabidly anticlerical. On the whole, public opinion indicated that the majority of the community remained loyal to the Emperor and the government's position. The Archbishop was unable to arouse any real support in the community.[54]

The scandal finally died: the issue had been decided by the government. Secular law regarding family rights was not to be violated by the church or church personnel. Yet even in its actions in this conflict, the authorities attempted to bridge the inherent conflict between church and state by exercising firmness with restraint, and was successful in this instance, at the local level.

However, Catholics' discomfort was compounded by the press's revelation of another scandal a few months later which involved a young adolescent girl, Elizabeth Linneweil, a target of overzealous Catholic women in Riom around 1860.[55] She was born in 1843 in Puy de Dôme, the daughter of an itinerant Jewish peddler and his mistress, in the neighborhood of the city of Clermont. The Linneweils were very poor and since their business necessitated continual travel, they had no permanent home. Therefore, the couple left the infant with a wet nurse who was paid six months in advance (a common practice in nineteenth century France). The nurse was also informed that the child was Jewish. The father promised to pay all additional expenses. However, because he was unable to meet all the financial obligations, the nurse went to Clermont, leaving the child at a hospice. In response to the civil authorities, the Jewish community assumed responsibility for the child and subsidized the costs. Subsequently, the Jewish leadership located a childless elderly couple named

Estener to assume the care of the baby. They became her foster parents, treating her as their own child, and renamed her Sarah Estener. Although they loved her and treated her as their own, they remained in touch with the Linneweils, informing them of their daughter's development and growth.[56]

As the child grew into adolescence, her foster parents became ill and their friends, a neighboring Catholic couple named Collat, took care of the young girl. When the Esteners died, the Collats became the executors of the estate, and offered Sarah the shelter of their home. Several months after the Esteners' deaths, Sarah's father, Meyer Linneweil, reclaimed his daughter and expressed a desire to bring her to his home. Lacking funds, he was forced to sell goods along the way, postponing a quick trip to Clermont and Riom.

The Collats, however, were determined to convert Elizabeth to their faith, and to accomplish that end, they arranged to separate the young girl from her family. They persuaded her that her parents had originally abandoned her, and that to return to them now "would result in her perdition or in prostitution."[57] She acceded to Mme. Collat's complicated plot to evade her father's custody. The distraught father searched all over Riom, and then sought help from the authorities. There was ample evidence that the Linneweils had kept in touch with their daughter's guardians, and the police were convinced that the Collat's tale of the Linneweils abandonment of Sarah was false.[58]

Elizabeth/Sarah had been sequestered secretly in a neighboring Carmelite nunnery. However, the nun's confessor and another priest had grave doubts about the legality of the Collat's activities. Furthermore, after extensive interviews, the priests observed that "She (Elizabeth) did not appear calm enough to undertake such a serious act. . . . From the tone of her language and the goals of the Jewess, there was a hint of doubt which led to my opposition (to the baptism)."[59] Her patrons refused to abide by their priests' doubts, and they persisted in their goal of conversion. They disguised her in different costumes, gave her various identities, and hid her in a variety of friends' homes and nunneries, among which was Theodore Ratisbonne's school of St. Mathilde de Sion.[60] The police finally located her, and she was returned to her parents. Reconciled with her uncle, father and mother, she discovered that her former protectors had lied. "I have learned to know and love my family who cherish me also."[61] The Collats and their friends were indicted and tried for the crime of kidnapping. They were exonerated of the criminal charges on a legal technicality (the Linneweils were not legally married, so family rights had not been violated), but they were declared guilty on the civil grounds of injuring the plaintiffs and were fined 3000 francs.[62]

The scandals discussed above played a relatively small role in the debates over the Roman question. Unfortunately, one of the undesirable side effects was that now the ultramontane's more defensive vision of Jews was reinforced as Jews and their community were perceived as the enemy of the faith, tradition, and Papal supremacy. However, the scandals, as already demonstrated, were useful in the derogation of clerical authority. As the tenuous alliance between the Church and Bonapartism was ruptured, the government responded by a cautious, yet inexorable movement toward liberalism, and one aspect of that development was the church-state struggle over the supervision of French schools. Even in this debate Jewish issues involved in the scandals of over zealous proselytization became an excuse for government policy.

Schools were the single most important modality in the transmission of value systems, knowledge, and cultural patterns. While educational institutions reflected the social system, they also were the active participants in the perpetuation and the maintenance of tradition. Whosoever controlled or dominated the schools would also transmit their cultural values. Therefore, in a France already divided over what constituted its true heritage, supervision of education became a paramount issue.

During the Ancien Regime, when altar and throne were firmly cemented, the church enjoyed a monopoly in the schools, supervising the entire educational structure from the colleges and universities to the petites écoles (which taught religion and some literacy to the poor). The throne was involved only with technical and military education. The revolution of 1789 destroyed clerical influence in the schools. Napoleon created state educational institutions, which remained somewhat the same until 1968, with modifications induced by the impetus of industrialization. In subsequent regimes the church had demanded and had been granted great influence in primary grades and in girls' schooling.[63] Custom had thus permitted teaching orders to enter the elementary grades and dominate all levels of the girls' schools. The reason was that most Catholics were firmly convinced that education should instill moral and ethical principles, and since France was a Catholic country, the church should control its content. Furthermore, government officials (whatever the regime) also believed that elementary education should function as a form of social control. Hence, stress was placed on inculcating values that would perpetuate the status quo. Therefore, logically, schools must teach morality, which in Catholic France, meant religion. This "religious" domination of the classroom did not pertain to the boys' schools, where it was more circumscribed, especially during liberal regimes.[64]

Arguments arose around questions of how *much* influence, how *much* religious instruction should be permitted in state schools. It was never an issue in any of the private religious schools (including Protestant and Jewish as well). However, the church, denied administrative power, continued to demand influence in the state system of schools. In contrast, the desired goal of the republicans was to exclude religion from the state schools (permitting parents to make their own arrangements for religious instruction). Most Frenchmen, however, felt the latter view was too extreme. They preferred compromise: ordinary subjects were to be taught objectively and secularly, while religious training was taught separately but kept as an integral part of the curriculum. Jews and Protestants provided their own instructors. This compromise was effective and acceptable in lycees and colleges.[65]

The primary schools and girls' schools were regarded differently. In 1833 the Guizot law placed "moral and religious instruction" in the forefront of their curriculum. The Revolution of 1848 seemed to have created a telling coup to the Catholic drive, but June Days with its social upheaval frightened the bourgeoisie. In their desire for social stability they backed the moderate Catholic Falloux law, which was also supported by Louis Napoleon as a part of his alliance with the Church. The Falloux law provided for the "liberty of education," meaning freedom for the Catholics to establish their own schools at the secondary level.

The result was not only the proliferation of Catholic schools, especially for girls, and rival lycees and colleges, but also a vast extension of Catholic influence in the primary schools. Religion, thus, came to play an important role in the majority of public as well as private schools. Prayer, catechism and church history were included in the curriculum in many of the state schools, varying from one region to another. Since there was a clear social demand for religious training, the major questions discussed by local officials became that of implementation: who supervised the inculcation?[66]

By 1850 about seventy percent of French children were enrolled in some school, and fifty-three percent were in public or state schools, usually taught by lay teachers. Regional differences, however, were widespread. Some communities, either to save money or for ideological reasons, permitted "religious" to teach in the primary schools. Government encouragement of religious orders also spurred this movement. Hence the convergence of the conservative temper of the French middle classes and the availability of the teaching orders enabled Catholic schools to expand in the years between 1850 and 1876, and to penetrate into the primary schools. However, the government insisted that Protestants and Jews provide their own religious training; although freethinkers and atheists were excluded from these laws and subsidies. In some cases over-zealous Catholics tried to subvert these restrictions and proselytize students.[67]

Although the Falloux law was a part of the pact between church and state, Louis Napoleon never intended to deliver state schools to the clergy. Fortoul, Minister of Education gradually asserted state control, altering part of the Falloux Law in 1854 by taking the power of teacher appointments away from the Municipal Councils and giving it to the prefects. Congregational schools, however, were free from government supervision and could move their personnel at will.

As the political debates after 1859 revealed the depth of ultramontane opposition, the government began to concern itself with the political loyalty in the Catholic schools. So long as the clergy had remained tactful and circumspect and refrained from open criticism of the regime, tacit cooperation was maintained between the church and state. However, Rouland, who succeeded Fortoul in 1856, was a fiery Gallican who sought to curb clerical authority in the primary schools by circumscribing the teaching congregations and expanding lay schools. Duruy, his successor, continued these policies even more forcefully, and also attempted to increase the number of state schools for girls. Political events increased the tempo of the state's restrictions. Both ministers were alarmed and irritated by what they deemed was the excessive political and religious propaganda of the conservatives who used pulpit and schools for their propaganda throughout their dioceses. Both ministers were reluctant to challenge the church head on, and they often used other issues as a rationale for their policies whose main aim was to reduce religious influence in French education. Jewish issues provided a convenient excuse for anticlerical legislation and administrative decision. Once again, ultramontanes' suspicions proved a reality as this government policy statement revealed:

> Many of the leaders and directors of the congregations have gone too far in claiming that the rights of proselytism should prevail over the civil

law. When minor children, reaching the age of
discernment, consent to abandon the beliefs of their
parents for the Catholic religion, they encourage
them, even by kidnapping them. . . . If this doctrine
were practiced with equal ardor by every religion
in France, it would cause intolerable perturbations.
Further, our legislation . . . sanctifies the rights of
the family. . . . The state must do its duty to prevent excesses of zeal because that is as damaging
to religion as it is menacing to the state.[68]

Later, the minister of education reiterated this policy, writing: "The
religious congregations presented a number of real dangers; their proselytization often destroyed families."[69] During the Second Empire the diverse views of church and state supervision over education were not resolved. Until 1880 the church had not relinquished its influence nor its
claims to it. It was most successful in girls' secondary education, but clerical teaching was circumscribed in higher education where the state exercised absolute authority.

Although the expressed policies of the government enacted in the
measures of Fortoul, Rouland, and Duruy sought to harness and channel
clerical influence, they did not silence conservative Catholics. Hence, a
long-term result of this conflict was that generations of some French children in some Catholic schools were taught that other religions were in
error and religious liberty was a grievous mistake. If Jewish and Protestant
beliefs were wrong, then it followed that such benighted groups ought
not to enjoy equal rights with true believers. Thus children imbibed bigotry and antisemitism; and conservatism was also strengthened, lending
it renewed vigor for the passionate controversies which would erupt in
the 1880s and 1890s. However, the lessons expostulated by the clergy reflected the personal position of leadership in the local region or in the
teaching orders. Since the church was disunited ideologically, their teaching reflected these differences. Nevertheless, a large number of Frenchmen
who had never seen a Jew were taught that they (Jews) were morally inferior, and participants in a dangerous alliance with free-masons and
other enemies of the church.

The quarrels over the fate of the Papacy seemed to abate after 1862.
However, French troops remained at Rome, protecting the Pope; a situation that the government wished to remedy. Negotiations, therefore, were

begun with the Italian government, in an attempt to preserve the Pope's temporal power in Rome, and yet evacuate French troops. Should such diplomatic efforts succeed, the Pope's safety had to be guaranteed so that the government would not alienate Catholic opinion. Because he wished to minimize the reassertion of ultramontane protest, Napoleon III justified his diplomacy by seizing every available opportunity to illustrate Papal abuse of human rights. An especially fortuitous occasion was presented in 1864 as the French were involved in negotiations for the September Convention. Another kidnapping analogous to the Mortara Affair took place in Rome.

A ten year old boy, Joseph Coen, had attracted the fancy of a priest who was shopping at the store of a shoemaker to whom the boy had been apprenticed. Impelled by the need to "save the child's soul," the priest asked the shoemaker to let Joseph deliver his shoes to him. As the Italian newspaper reported :

> The young Jew repairs without suspicion to a
> customer of his master; he is received there with
> honeyed kindness, is treated to a ride in his car-
> riage, and driven to Catechumens, where he is
> shut up, despite his cries and protestations.[70]

The parents were distressed when their child did not come home, and when they learned of his whereabouts, they became frantic. The mother's cries, the father's exhortations were denied, and the family was forced to leave Rome. The boy was baptized on 29 September 1864 and given a new name. His godfather was the illustrious Comte de Maistre.[71] The boy disappeared from history and nothing further was known of his development.

The protests which arose in response to this kidnapping were similar to those expressed earlier in 1858. However, there were some differences. Although indignation ran high, there was no hope that the Pope would return the boy to his parents. Indeed, much of the press comment both in France and abroad centered on the presence of French troops in Rome, and their role in the maintenance of Papal power.

In London, the *Daily News* complained that for the second time in six years the Papacy's abduction of a child "violated sacred rights" of paternity and also noted: "This child of ten years has astonished all who heard him by answering the most abstract questions in theology, though he had

never read a Christian book! . . ."72   A Viennese paper vigorously protested that this new "Mortara" affair was morally reprehensible and a deed of
savage barbarism.73 The Paris correspondent of the London *Times* linked
the Affair to the September Convention, saying: "The Pope has hitherto
been able to set at defiance alike his protectors and his countrymen. The
protectors being withdrawn . . . he will no longer be suffered to enjoy the
delights of small persecutions . . . and kidnapping of Jewish children will
be remembered as a practice of the good old times when infallibility re-
posed on French bayonets."74   In France, the anticlerical press demanded
that the French government protest energetically. *Siècle* asked the rhetorical question: "Can we protect at Rome what we do not tolerate at
home?"75 *L'Union*, a Catholic journal, responded by deploring French protests at Rome, declaring that France should not interfere in the sovereign
affairs of another state.76

The affair had erupted during the delicate negotiations over the September Convention and the French government, as its custom, was willing
to use the issue to promote its program.   An article appeared in the *Journal
des Débats* which demanded a strong French response to the Papacy. The
remedy suggested was: "Let our army be withdrawn from Rome and the
temporal government of the Pope abandoned to itself."77 Rumors
abounded that this editorial had been inserted by the government, to prepare the public for the eventual acceptance of the Convention.78

Jewish protests in the press were as vociferous and angry as in 1858,
but they, too, acknowledged the futility of recriminations. A circular
(similar to the one of 1858) was sent to Rome,79 but it had no effect. Jewish leadership, now committed to international cooperation, and joint
action, recognized that a mission to Rome would be useless—as it had
been in 1858. Nevertheless, the Jewish communities did express their in-
dignation.80 The French government also protested, and once again, emphasized the fact to Cardinal Antonelli, that an adverse decision by the
Pope would only rebound to the benefit of the anticlerical foes of the temporal power.   Antonelli responded by requesting a forty day respite before giving a final answer.   However, both sides were aware that the
Coen boy was a subject of the Pope and the kidnapping was in fact, an
internal matter.   The French government, as in 1858, could accomplish very
little because "the official intervention of France would not be admissible
according to international law."81

The Papacy's decision denying the parents' request for custody was
based on the rationalization published in the semiofficial paper *Giornale di*

Roma. According to the paper, the boy, apprenticed to a Catholic shoe-maker, was so overwhelmed by the kindness of his master and his customers, that he desired to convert to Catholicism. He begged and cajoled to be taken to a priest, and finally convinced both his master and the priest of his sincerity. He was further interrogated by a cardinal in the presence of the Roman governor and two other officials. The commission was convinced by the boy's ardor. They offered to repeat the examination before the father and the Secretary of the Jewish Community, both of whom refused to attend. The account concluded that "the falsehoods, calumnies, and the outrages of the press will never turn away the Holy See from the path marked out by justice."[82] *L'Opinione* of Turin denied this account declaring that in an audience with the Pope the boy cried and asked to return home to his parents.[83] *Le Monde* was one of the few French papers that sustained the Papal position by translating an article from *Correspondance di Roma* which castigated the protesters as part of "the Revolution" that desired to revive the Mortara Affair. The article continued by averring that despite the conspiracies of London and Turin, the press and various diplomats, the Vicar of Christ remained firm in his resolve to save souls.[84] Taconet, the editor, then pleaded that children should have freedom of religion, for "if a non-Catholic child is touched by grace why shouldn't he enter the Catholic religion?"[85]

The government had negotiated the September Convention whose provisions had provided for the withdrawal of French troops from Rome; in return the Italians would transfer their capital to Florence. Both the adversaries and the partisans of the temporal power perceived the Convention as surreptitious abandonment of the Pope. The past failures to exert influence upon official diplomacy, the subtle attacks upon the church by the government, and the passivity of the parishes' response, prompted churchmen to act with caution. Moreover, another scandal had brought further disrepute to the Papacy, for once again, as in 1858, most Catholics were sympathetic to the Coen parents. Hence popular opinion was resigned to official decisions, so long as the Pope remained in Rome.[86]

Despite the negotiations of the September Convention, the Roman Question continued to plague the government as Garibaldi's attack upon Rome annulled the earlier settlement. Public interest was less intense as the Prussian threat became more obvious. Debates in the press became more diversified and less strident about the Pope's temporal power, as the government's press policies became more liberal. Antisemitism, arising in the polemics of the Roman question, remained potent. Both the extreme right and the left, using stereotypes and older prejudices, became more strident as the emerging prominence of important Jewish public figures became more visible. These personalities will be examined in the next chapter.

1 Mérimée to Panizzi, Paris, 23 October 1861, Prosper Mérimée, *Lettres à M. Panizzi 1850-1870*, (Paris, 1871), I, 231.

2 Phayer, 113-28.

3 G. de Vaux and Henri Riondrel, *Vie du Père Jean Roothan, 1785-1853*, (Paris: Lethielleux, 1935), 102-08.

4 Phayer, 130; Claude Savart, "Cent ans après: Les apparitions mariales en France au XIXe siècle, un ensemble?" *Revue d' Histoire de la Spiritualité*, 48 (1972): 205-20.

5 Jean Guitton, *La conversion de Ratisbonne*, (Paris: Wesmaelo-Charlier, 1964).

6 Guitton, 7; *Encyclopedia Judaica*, (New York, 1972), 13, col. 1, 1571; c. f. Theodore Ratisbonne, *Quelque mots sur l'Affaire de la famille Bluth*, (Paris, 1861), 10-11; *La Vérité Israélite*, March 186.

7 Cohen, *La Promotion des juifs*, I, 719-20; c. f. *Archives Israélites*, *L'Univers Israélite*, and *La Vérité*, wrote many editorials excoriating proselytizing by Christians and especially that of apostates such as the Ratisbonnes.

8 Central Israelite Consistory to Minister of Religion, Paris, 19 March 1845, AN, F 19, 11031.

9 Minister of Religion to Minister of War, 8 January 1860, AN, F 19, 11031.

10 Minister of Religion to Minister of Interior, 13, 19 April, AN, 19, 11031; *Times*, (London), 12 November 1858; *Archives Israélites*, January 1859; Central Israelite Consistory to Minister of religion, Paris, 3 June 1877, AN, F 19, 11031.

11 *La Vérité Israélite*, 18 September 1861; *Archives Israélites*, March 1858; Prefect of Bouche-du-Rhone, 20 March 1861, upheld the work of missionary Abbé Bauer despite the accusations of antisemitism by the Consistory, AN, F 19, 11031.

12 *L'Opinion Nationale*, 7 March 1861.

13 Ibid.; Pre-trial Interrogation, 10 October 1861, AN, F 19, 7879.

14 Adolph Bluth to Rouland, Paris, 19 January 1862, AN, F 19, 7879. A younger brother, Louis, was baptized secretly at the age of eight by Abbé Mallet without the parents' permission or knowledge.

15 *L'Opinion Nationale*, 7, 8, 9, 10 March 1861 recounted the entire story and reproduced the entire transcript of the Mallet trial.

16 Ratisbonne to Maria Siona, Paris, 26 November 1855; Declaration of Louise Bluth, 30 May 1860, AN, F 19, 7879.

[17] Ibid., *L'Opinion Nationale*, 7 March 1861.

[18] Pre-trial deposition, 1861, AN, F 19, 7879.

[19] Elizabeth Bluth to parents, 1861, AN, F 19, 7879; *La Vérité Israélite*, 7 March 1861.

[20] Rouland to Napoleon III, Paris, 29 May 1861, AN, F 19, 7879; c. f. Lita Schwartz and Natalie Isser, "Psycho-historical Perceptions of Involuntary Conversion," *Jewish Social Studies*, 14 (1979): 35-60. The effects of brainwashing relevant to involuntary religious conversion are discussed.

[21] Taxile Delord, *Histoire du Second Empire*, (Paris,1869-70), II, 210-13.

[22] *L'Opinion Nationale*, 23 April 1861; *La Vérité Israélite*, 28 March, 25 April 1861.

[23] Ratisbonne, *Quelques mots sur l'affaire de la famille Bluth.*

[24] Theodore-Marie Ratisbonne, *Ratisbonne fondateur de la société des prêtres et de la con-grégation des religieuses de Notre-Dame de Sion*, I, 128-29.

[25] *Le Constitutionnel*, 4, 5 March; 15 April 1861.

[26] *L'Opinion Nationale*, 6, 9, 10 March 1861.

[27] *Le Siècle*, 6, 10 March 1861.

[28] *Le Monde*, 18 March 1861.

[29] *La Gazette de France*, 11 March 1861.

[30] *L'Union*, reproduced in *Le Monde*, 10 March 1861.

[31] *Le Journal des Villes et des Campagnes*, in *Le Monde*, 14 March 1861.

[32] La Gorce, IV, 124.

[33] Maurain, 464; c.f. François Dutacq, *Gustave Rouland, Ministre de l'Instruction publique 1856-1863*, (Tulle, 1910), 276.

[34] Rouland to Napoleon III, 29 May 1861, AN, F 19, 7879.

[35] Prefect of Nord to Rouland, 6 July 1861; Procureur General to Garde des Sceaux, 14 July 1861; Paris, Minister of Justice to Rouland, 8 July 1861, AN, F 19, 6313

[36] Archbishop of Cambrai to Rouland, 9 April 1861, AN, F 19, 7879; c. f. *Mémorial de Lille*, 8 December 1861.

[37] Maurain, 467.

[38] Archbishop of Cambrai to Rouland, 9 April 1861, AN, F 19, 7879

[39] Mayor of Douai to Rouland (no date). Extract of deliberations of the Municipal Council of Douai, 11 September 1862, AN, F 19, 6313.

[40] *Moniteur Universel*, 10 October 1861; *Le Constitutionnel*, 10 October 1861

[41] Archbishop of Cambrai to Rouland, Cambrai, 23 October 1861, AN, F19, 6313.

[42] *Mémorial de Lille*, 15 December 1861. The archbishop stated this goal in a letter to the editor.

[43] Circular of Msgr. the Archbishop of Cambrai to the clergy of his diocese on the occasion of the affair of the Sisters of Sainte-Union.

[44] *L'Émancipation de Cambrai*, 1 December 1861; *Propagateur de Lille*, 29 November 1861.

[45] "Polemic" of the press, AN, F 19, 6313.

46 Ibid.; Prefect of the Nord to Rouland, Lille, 8 December 1861, AN, F 19, 6313.

47 Ibid.

48 Prefect of the Nord to Rouland, Lille, 27 December 1861, AN, F 19, 6313; 26, 27 December 1861; *Mémorial de Lille,* 26, 27 December 1861.

49 Ibid.

50 *Mémorial de Lille,* 8 January 1862.

51 Prefect of the Nord to Rouland, telegram, Lille, 19 January 1862, AN, F, 19, 6313.

52 *L'Echo du Nord,* 16 January 1862; *Mémorial de Lille,* 26 January 1862.

53 Natalie Isser, "The Mallet Affair, A Case Study in Scandal," *Revue des Etudes juives,* 138 (Fall, 1979): 291-305.

54 Procureur report, Douai, 1861, AN, BB30, 377.

55 Elisabeth Linneweil, deposition, Puy de Dôme, AD, Haut Marne; *Archives Israélites,* November 1861; c. f. N. Isser, "The Linneweil Affair," *Adolescence,* 19 (1984): 630-31.

56 Estener to Linneweil, Puy de Dôme, 19 September 1856; Deposition of Joseph Marx, 1861, Acte d'accusation, AD, Haut Marne.

57 Deposition of Elisabeth Linneweil, 1861, AD, Haut Marne; *Archives Israélites,* November 1861.

58 Ibid.

59 Deposition of Father Rouisson, 1861, AD, Haut Marne.

60 Deposition of Elisabeth Linneweil, 1861, AD, Haut Marne.

61 Ibid.

62 Mémoire, Puy de Dôme, 1861, AD, Haut Marne; Isser, "The Linneweil Affair," 629-42; Cohen, *La promotion des juives,* II, 715.

63 R. D. Anderson, *Education in France, 1848-1870,* (Oxford: Clarendon Press, 1975), 105-27; Joseph Moody, *French Education Since Napoleon,* (Syracuse: Syracuse University Press, 1978).

64 Patrick J. Harrigan, "The Church and Pluralistic Education: the Development of Teaching in French Catholic Secondary Schools, 1859-1870," 64, *Catholic Historical Review* (April, 1978): 185-213; Patrick Harrigan, "Social and Political Implications of Catholic Secondary Education during the Second French Empire," *Societas,* 6-7 (Winter, 1976): 41-59; c. f. Pierre Zind, *L'Enseignement religieux dans l'instruction primaire publique en France de 1850 à 1873,* (Lyon: Centre historique de Catholicisme, 1976).

65 Pierre Zind, "La religion dans les lycees sous le regime de la Loi Falloux 1859-17" in Donald N. Baker and Patrick J. Harrigan, *The Making of Frenchmen: Current Directions in the History of Education in France, 1679-1879,* (Waterloo: Historical Reflections Press, 1980), 261-73

66 Marie-Bernadette Bédry, "L'instruction primaire dans l'arrondissement de Toulouse sous le Second Empire," *Annales du Midi,* 91 (no. 144, 1979): 468-71.

[67] Moody, 67-70; Harrigan, 41-59; Zind, *L'enseignement religieux*, 306-12; c. f. Sandra Horvath-Peterson, *Victor Duruy and French Education*, (Baton Rouge: Louisiana State Univ. Press, 1984).

[68] *Moniteur Universel*, 26, 27 December 1861; c. f. Cohen, *La promotion des juives*, II, 746-47.

[69] Ibid., 12 March 1865.

[70] *Opinione* (Turin), 26 July, 3 August 1864 cited in *Jewish Chronicle* (London), 12 August 1864; *L'Independance Belge*, 29 July 1864 cited in *L'Univers Israélite*, September 1864.

[71] *Patriota Cattolica*, (Bologna) cited in *Archives Israélites*, December 1864.

[72] *Daily News*, (London), 31 August 1864, 28 September 1864.

[73] *Le Constitution*, (Vienna), cited in the *Jewish Chronicle*, 30 September 1864.

[74] *Times*, (London), 6 October 1864.

[75] *Siècle*, 13 August 1864.

[76] *L'Union* in AN, F 19, 1937.

[77] *Journal des Débats* cited in *Jewish Chronicle*, 2 September 1864

[78] Ibid.

[79] *L'Univers Israélite*, October 1864.

[80] *Jewish Chronicle*, (London), 9 September 1864; c. f. *Archives Israélites, L'Univers Israélite*, September-December 1864.

[81] Affair Coen, 23 August 1864, AN, F19, 1937.

[82] *L'Opinione*, (Turin), cited in *Archives Israélites*, November 1864.

[83] *Le Monde*, 11 August 1864.

[84] Ibid., 2 August 1864; the editor of the *Univers Israélites* observed that Catholics protested proselytization and harassment of their children in Protestant states, *L'Univers Israélite*, October 1864.

[85] Ibid.

[86] Maurain, 702-03; Procureur reports, AN, BB30, 370.

Chapter V

Acceptance or Toleration?

By the 1840s and 50s, many Jews (especially the Sephardic ones) had become wealthy and many achieved prominence in French banking, literature, music, art, and science. Indeed, their very success made them highly visible, and served to reinforce stereotypes and prejudices in French society at large. Nevertheless, they enjoyed protection from the government, and wide acceptance in many stratas of French life. They were and are still a small minority in France; as such they often endured a feeling of isolation and apprehension about antisemitism. Their success was also a reflection of their perceived inferior position and their sense of separateness which was abetted by episodes of humiliation or discrimination. According to David Landes, the Protestants and Jews were "outsiders" and thus driven to seek dignity and status within the majority culture by attaining success in business and the arts.[1] What was even more interesting about some of these Jews was that they were in the forefront of French modernization and development: a fact that further irritated those that deplored change.

The most prominent and important individual in the Jewish community was Achille Fould, who was minister of state from 1852 to 1860, senator and twice minister of finance (1849-1852, 1861-1867). He was born in Paris in 1800, the son of the founder of a family bank, Beer Léon Fould. With his older brother Benoît, he entered the family business after an extensive education, as was customary. While Benoît managed the bank and became involved with high finance, Achille turned his attention to politics. In 1842 he was elected to the Chamber of Deputies from Tarbès (Hautes-Pyrénées), where he supported the Guizot Ministry. After the fall of the Orleans Monarchy, he ran as an Orleanist deputy and was elected to the Constituent Assembly from Paris in the by-elections of July 1848. Frightened by the unrest and social upheaval of the June Days he, as many other Orleanists, rallied to Louis Napoleon as a part of the party of order. He became the finance minister in the Prince President's government and accepted the coup d'état of 2 December 1851, but he resigned in January of the following year in protest against the Orleans confiscations. In spite of Fould's disapproval of his policy, the emperor appointed him to the Senate on 26 January 1852.

Achille Fould was the first Jew to be named to the Senate. He married a Protestant woman who claimed that he embraced her faith, and indeed his children were raised as Christians. However, some contemporary opinion was that he had not changed his religion (although his widow had him buried as a Protestant). During his lifetime he supported a small synagogue and the poor on his estate at Tarbes, but unlike his brother Benoît, he evidenced no other belief in Judaism.[2] Nevertheless, as an important government official he defended Jewish interests such as eradicating antisemitic sentiments in the theater. His political leanings generally were supportive of Jewish interests. In the matter of tariffs he was a protectionist, and in economics, a fiscal conservative (interests which were not necessarily Jewish ones), but in church matters he was a Gallican, and in the Roman Question he favored the withdrawal of French troops from Rome: positions supported by the Jewish community. The result was that ultramontanes hated him for his beliefs, and because he was a Jew.

In November 1860 Fould resigned from the Ministry of State but he remained in the good graces of the Emperor. Napoleon III granted Fould the grand cross of the Legion of Honor in March of 1865. In December 1861 he was once again appointed Minister of Finance; he pursued a very conservative fiscal policy as he attempted to balance the budget. He resigned his position in 1867, and died soon afterwards. His role as a public official was distinguished although historians debate whether his orthodox monetary policies were good for the French economy.

Fould was accepted by the Emperor in the highest society of Paris; he represented the assimilated Jew who, although still loyal to his community, had in reality begun to move into the majority. His brother Benoît, on the other hand, remained a leader of Jews and faithful to Judaism. He continued the banking firm and became associated with the other leading bankers of the Second Empire in the formation of the Crédit Mobilier.[3]

Other important bankers of this period were the Pereires and the Rothschilds. Baron James de Rothschild was the symbol of the "parasitical Jewish rich banker" described by Toussenel. As the youngest son of Mayer Amshel Rothschild of Frankfurt, he was sent to Paris in 1811, where he founded the French bank which became preeminent. During the July Monarchy, he was especially influential in financing the railways of France.

However, his association with the Orleans dynasty put his interests under suspicion during the Revolution of 1848. The triumph of Louis Napoleon placed the Rothschilds at a disadvantage in their emerging rivalry with the banking interests of the Foulds and the Pereires.

The Pereires, Isaac and Jules, were born and raised in Bordeaux. As many young Jews of the time, they were attracted to Saint-Simonian teachings.[4] Influenced by new notions of public finance and borrowing, the brothers engaged in vast bold entrepreneurial enterprises, most notably the development of French railroads (with Rothschild cooperation). They enjoyed, however, their greatest achievements during the Second Empire. The Emperor, desirous of encouraging the rebuilding of cities of France, and expanding the French economy, regarded the Pereires' proposals with sympathy and thus enabled them to found one of the banks which expanded credit facilities: the Crédit mobilier with which Benoît Fould was involved. During the twenty years of Napoleon III's reign the Pereires contributed to the port as well as to the urban development of Marseilles and Paris; they built successful railways in Austria, Spain, and Switzerland; and they supported the Anglo-French treaty. They were in favor of low tariffs, cheap money, limited liability, reform of the Bank of France, the expansion of banking facilities, and greater use of government loans rather than taxes. These ideas and their over-speculation in many of their enterprises earned them the opposition of the Rothschilds, Magne, Baroche, Mocquard, Rouher, Achille Fould, and other conservatives. Gradually Napoleon III began to lean toward James Rothschild's policies, a sentiment which was cemented in his visit to Ferrières, the Rothschild estate.

The Emperor came on a visit to the Rothschilds in December 1862 accompanied by A. Fould, Walewski, Lord Cowley, and other important officials. The occasion, though merely social, marked the end of the Pereires' influence and ascendency of a more conservative economic policy: the triumph of Haute Banque which, however, had coopted some of the more expansionist policies advocated by its rivals. What was equally important was the fact that the Emperor and his entourage had participated in a breakfast and hunting party that was duly reported and noted with great detail in the press. It marked the social acceptance of Jews at the highest levels.[5] James Rothschild, forced to copy methods of the Crédit mobilier, maintained his international connections with the rest of his family. He also kept his Jewish connections, and his children married within the Jewish community. The Pereires were ousted from economic influence in the administration, and faced total defeat when their Crédit mobilier fared poorly in 1866-67 (caused partially by bad management and poor financial judgement). The bank was saved from failure by the Bank of France, but the Pereires were forced to resign. Though the Pereires lost their economic influence, they, at the request of the Emperor, ran for election to the Legislative Body in 1863 and were duly elected. The next year both men were awarded the rank of officer in the Legion of Honor. It was however, during the elections in 1863, and later in 1869, that antisemitism became especially active in local political affairs.[6]

The Pereires, although they had totally assimilated, accepted their loyalty to Judaism as a formality rather than a commitment. Nevertheless, they continued to contribute to Jewish institutions and maintained a semblance of leadership with the Jewish communal organizations. Hence, when they ran for election, they were identified as Jews and endured antisemitic attacks by their opponents. The opposition candidates in the Pyrénées-orientales in 1863 were mostly legitimist and ardent clericals. The ultramontanes threw their support to the opposition and in the campaign did not hesitate to employ vicious antisemitism against the government candidates. A Catholic priest, in a scurrilous pamphlet, revived the fable of ritual murder when he (despite all the proofs to the contrary) declared the "Damascus" murder in 1840 of a Capuchin priest was a such a crime. The ultramontanes asserted that because the Pereires did not believe in the divinity of Christ or the the virgin birth, they were unfit to serve in the Legislative Body. Such attacks were approved and supported by the Bishop of Carcassonne himself.[7]

Again in 1869, Isaac Pereire was subjected to some of the same attacks when he again ran for office in the department of Aude. He ran against a candidate who had the support of landed notables and especially the clergy, who were just as determined in this department as their colleagues had been earlier, to defeat Isaac Pereire. The election became sharply divided between the legitimist clericals and the liberals. Pereire based his campaign upon the themes of progress and economic development, while asserting his opponent was devoted to the principles of the ancien regime. Many on the left resented him because he was the government-sponsored candidate and because of his banking connections. However, Pereire was now handicapped by the failure of the Crédit mobilier, which was duly noted in the *Courrier de l'Aude*, 18 May 1869; and by the fact that his opponent was a native of the region. He was the "foreigner" and the "Jew;" phrases which were either chanted by the crowds or pasted on the walls. The priests, on instruction of their bishop, were asked to combat the candidacy of a "Jew hostile to the Church," whose election would be a "shame" for the community. He won the election by a narrow victory, but the results were annulled by the Legislative Body, citing electoral irregularities.[8] The election was based on electoral abuses which his party and local officials had perpetrated and which was common practice in the earlier years of the regime, but by 1869 the Legislative Body no longer regarded them with complacency. Isaac Pereire's victory fell victim to emerging power of the Liberal Empire.[9] Nevertheless, the campaign once more illustrated how Jews and the Roman question had become intertwined. For the clergy were convinced by the arguments over the fate of the Mortara and Coen children, and other debates, that the Jews were engaged in a vicious conspiracy to deprive the Pope of all his temporal possessions. They, therefore, would oppose any Jew's election, no matter how conservative, because he could not support their ultramontane positions.

Other notable figures who aroused conservative Catholic antisemitism were those most often associated with newspaper publication. Prominent Jewish bankers also soon became involved with the press, for it was during this period that newspapers expanded to become mass organs of communication and big business ventures.[10] Moïse Millaud and Jules Mirès were the most notable of these entrepreneurs during the Second Empire.

Like the Pereires and Jules Mirès,[11] Millaud was born in Bordeaux (in February 1813). His family were merchants of modest means, and he did not receive an extensive education. Driven by ambition and grandiose dreams, he left for Paris in 1836 to seek his fortune. He founded several small papers whose existence was very brief. Finally, in 1838 he founded a paper, *Négociateur*, which proved to be the turning point in his search for success. For this newspaper marked the joining of the press and finance: the first journal devoted only to reporting business affairs. Later, in 1848, collaborating with Mirès, he purchased the *Journal des chemins de fer*, an enterprise which proved to be financially rewarding. In 1839 he also experimented with a paper devoted only to crime and the courts in partnership with Léo Lespès (*L'audience*). This paper gave him notoriety though it lasted only until 1845.

During the revolution of 1848 he founded a paper, *La Liberté*, which was soon to be suppressed because of its support for Louis Napoleon. He then went into partnership with Mirès, buying several newspapers and founding a bank, the Caisse des Actions Réunies. He made a handsome profit and left the group; his place was taken by Félix Solar (another Jew from Bordeaux) who with Mirès joined to transform the bank into the

Caisse Générale des Chemins de Fer. Though Millaud continued to speculate in a variety of businesses and banks, his more important role was in the field of journalism where he was directly involved with the development of the newspaper as an agency of the mass media.

In December 1856 he acquired *La Presse* from Emile de Girardin but when his various financial holdings foundered he sold his papers to Solar, who also acquired *Journal des chemins de fer* from Mirès. But Millaud, determined to continue innovation in publishing, launched *Le Petit Journal* in February 1863. He achieved more completely the earlier experiment of a large daily that Girardin had started in *La Presse*. *Petit Journal* was published in tabloid form and was sold by the individual copy for five centimes daily. Millaud avoided partisan political opinion by organizing his paper around the publishing of "news" and paid advertising.[12] The paper was enormously successful. He continued to acquire papers and both his son and nephew aided in their management. He dabbled in the theater, but in 1869 he again encountered financial difficulties and was forced to sell *Le Petit Journal*. He died in October 1871.[13]

Félix Solar, like Mirès and Millaud, was an editor and sometimes journalist, but also he was an active and engaged businessman. He began his career as the editor of the *Courrier de Bordeaux*, then went to Paris where he studied law. In 1845, collaborating with Granier de Cassagnac (a future prominent Bonapartist journalist), he founded the paper *L'Epoque*. He was essentially a conservative devoted to the policies of Guizot. He then became the editor of *Patrie* and moved to the *Messager de l'Assemblée*, which disappeared after the coup d'état of 1851. He became Mirès' partner both in business and other newspaper enterprises, and in 1856 he acquired *La Presse*. In addition to his reputation as a journalist, businessman, and editor, he became famous as a bibliophile; his collection, which he sold in 1860, contained rare and precious works. However, his connection with Mirès proved disastrous. He was the co-defendent in the trial during the Mirès scandal. He was found guilty, condemned to five years in prison and fined three thousand francs. He fled to Italy to avoid his sentence and returned to France in 1869, after Mirès' appeal led to his exoneration. Solar then became the editor of *Libre Échange* until his death in November 1870.[14]

The careers of these men were ample evidence that France granted genuine freedom to its Jews after the end of the Restoration. Unlike other communities in Europe, Jews did not need to convert in order to achieve political, economic, or social acceptance. Entrance to schools and the equality of treatment was generally the norm and enforced by law.[15]

Jews entered and participated in every aspect of French life, as shown by the careers of the aforesaid men. They could, as many did, sunder their close relationship with the Jewish community, but in other examples such as Michel Goudchaux, Adolph Crémieux, Benoît Fould, and Alexander Weill, they continued as leaders in their consistories and charitable organizations. The overall result was that conversions were relatively rare; Offenbach and the Ratisbonnes converted for personal and psychological reasons, not because it was necessary to achieve acceptance. These leaders of enterprise not only accumulated great fortunes, but they were attracted to and enjoyed the society of the most important intellectual, political and literary figures of the Second Empire. They gave splendid parties; they were renowned for their costly and important art collections.[16] And when they wished, their children were able to marry within the aristocratic families, as Jules Mirès daughter did, in spite of her father's lower social origins and the later scandals.

There was, however, a darker side to this picture. The great success and affluence of these new Jewish families, who maintained their connections with one another and frequently intermarried, disturbed some in French society. French business enterprise in the nineteenth century was generally organized on a family basis. Enhancement of the family prosperity meant that the family could use their position to provide careers for their children in politics, or even use their success to arrange good marriages. From the seventeenth century the Protestants had gained influence in the banking houses, shipping, commission, and cotton manufacturing.[17] Now Jews, too, had developed newer banking institutions, and had gained access to the press. These sources of power meant that Jews enjoyed almost as much influence as the Protestants.

To those ultramontanes who had long been convinced that France was gravely threatened by modernism and revolution, the rise to eminence of these Jews represented the confirmation of their worst fears and beliefs. The Jews, Saint-Simonians, Protestants, and Masons were all united in conspiratorial opposition to the Pope. They were convinced that the Mortara Affair which had been so harmful to their cause, had been orchestrated by the "Jewish press" and international Jewish bankers. If the right's stereotypes of the "Jewish press" were exemplified by Millaud, Solar, Mirès and lesser journalists such as Desiré Pollonnais and Alexandre Weill, the socialists also found equally powerful images to sustain their misdirected prejudices: The Mirès scandal, the failure of the Crédit mobilier, and the influence of the Rothschilds.

Alphonse Toussenel had already used James Rothschild as a symbol of the "Jewish capitalist," but a new spate of pejorative articles emerged, such as the one which appeared in *Le Nain Jaune* on July 1865. Entitled "Money Men," it was a veiled attack on Jewish entrepreneurs. George Duchêne's socialist rhetoric was even more openly harsh in its condemnation of Jewish businessmen, especially in later pamphlets. A brochure entitled *Vie de Judas* was removed from the book shelves by the government at the request of the consistory because it contained blatantly cruel caricatures of Jews.[18] The new Jewish men like the Pereires, Mirès and others figured also in the works of such diverse writers as Ernest Feydeau,[19] J. B. Capefigue,[20] and far more virulently in the works of Edouard Drumont during the Third Republic. [21]

There were other aspects of French artistic and intellectual life in which Jews had enjoyed great success. The theater was an arena in which the names of Rachel (the great actress), Eugène Manuel, Offenbach (who converted to Catholicism) and Meyerbeer were dominant. Jews also excelled in medicine and other scientific scholarship. However, it was in academic scholarship, the study of philology and ancient Semitic languages, that Jews dominated. Men such as Adolph Franck, Joseph Derenburg, Joseph Halévy, and Jules Oppert occupied distinguished chairs in many universities in Paris and the provinces. Oppert was not French; he had emigrated to France because he could not teach in a university in the German states. These Jews distinguished themselves and their departments; they specialized not only in Hebrew, but also Syrian, Arabic, and ancient history. The most renowned of these scholars was Solomon Munk. They brought great luster to the University of Paris, which became famous for the high quality of its mid-eastern studies.

It was largely from these groups that inspiration was gathered for one of the more passionate debates of the Second Empire. That controversy raged over Ernest Renan, also an admired and brilliant scholar of mid-eastern languages. Renan wrote the celebrated *Vie de Jésus* (1863) and *Saint-Paul et sa mission* (1867). The former book evoked enormous outrage from both Catholics and Jews. The latter work enraged Jewish writers as well, but the impassioned dialogue centered upon his *Vie de Jésus*. That book was a sensation, because its basic theme denied the divinity of Jesus.

Renan, at the time, was a world-wide recognized and accomplished "Orientalist." He was also renowned as an astute critic. He was not an atheist, but deeply committed to his church and traditional morality. Though he declared in his book that Jesus was a human being, he remained close to Christian traditional values. He characterized Jesus as a great sage and noble personality—a divine human being—but still "frail, fallible and mortal." Jesus was the most transcendent of human beings though Renan claimed that Jesus never dreamed of being an "Incarnation of God" because "that notion was foreign to the Jewish mind." Nevertheless, "Jesus was intoxicated with such infinite love that it loosened the heavy chain which holds the mind captive."[22]

Renan's study of Jesus was thus that of a historical figure, a Jewish man, born in Palestine. He treated the Gospels as historical sources and discarded the notion of miracles. His biography and subsequent works resulted in a more critical and natural evaluation of Christ. However, although Renan recognized the Judaic roots of Jesus and claimed that the Torah or Jewish law offered high ideals for daily living, he, too, declared that the Mosaic law was rigid. He further maintained that although Jewish teachers offered high ideals, only Jesus had effectively preached them. Despite his radical challenge to the church on the divinity of Christ, he remained loyal to Catholic teaching in relating the story of the crucifixion. In the traditional manner, he condemned the Pharisees by writing: "It was, then, neither Tiberious nor Pilate who condemned Jesus. It was the old Jewish party, it was the Mosaic law." To his credit, Renan did insist that it was wrong to make modern Jews suffer for deicide. He condemned Christian intolerance, but weakened his denunciation by stating that intolerance was not a Christian fact. "It is a Jewish fact . . . introduced by Judaism which has given the example of an immutable dogma armed with the sword." And he concluded by repeating traditional Christian dogma: ". . . The religion of Jesus is in some respects the final religion. . . . All that is done outside of this great Christian tradition is barren. . . ."[23]

In the main, because his thesis supported the Jewish view of Jesus of Nazareth, Caraguel in the *Charivari* ironically commented that: "M. Renan does not admit the divinity of Jesus; in his eyes he is only a man, though a divine man. . . . This thesis is not new, and without going very far we elbow every day very honorable people who no more believe in the divinity of Jesus than himself, who expect the Messiah, and who have been salaried by the state to teach this doctrine in their synagogues!"[24] However, Renan used language and verbiage that was unfriendly to the Jews. Indeed, he reflected the prejudice and Christian beliefs about Jews and Judaism which were prevalent at that time and are still entertained among some Christian communities today. Although Renan examined the Gospels in a critical fashion by questioning the accuracy of the writers and their records, he still mistranslated many Hebrew words and sentences, and he showed a complete misunderstanding of ancient Judaism and modern Jewish practices. It was to these inaccuracies and misunderstandings that the Jewish community directed its most acute and bitter critical comments.

The Jewish pens were as acerbic in their criticisms as were the Catholic conservatives. If Catholics were concerned with Renan undermining faith, Jews turned their attention to his prejudices. They commented that such canards and inaccuracies were unworthy of a scholar of such renown as Renan. As one writer said: "He (Renan) heaps upon us reproaches, the very nature of which call forth a smile of pity on the lips of every friend." For instance, the writer continues, Renan says: "With enormous faults, being hard, egotistical, cruel, narrow minded, subtle, sophisticated, the Jewish people is nevertheless, the author of the finest comment of disinterested enthusiasm of which history speaks." The Jewish critic assailed Renan by citing Torah and other Jewish laws which command charity and speak to abnegation and devotion to humanity. Rhetorically he demanded, "Where are the Jewish acts of cruelty? Open the pages of history and Jews appeared as the victims and not the persecutors!" Pointing to Renan's accusation that Jews were intolerant, the writer pointedly said: Jewish law at no time ever "compelled strangers to embrace its (Jewish) religion, nor did it pass laws of exclusion." Jews never established ghettos for pagans nor promulgated laws of exclusion. And Judaism did not accept the idea that "beyond the church there is no salvation, for it proclaimed that the pious of all nations will enjoy everlasting life." The editorial writer of the *Archives Israélites* attacked the assumption repeated by Renan that Jews regarded their enemies with hatred (unlike Christians) because the word "neighbor" in Judaism refers to only a co-religionist. Cahen (the editor) reprovedRenan for mistranslating the Hebrew phrase because the word "neighbor" in Hebrew applies without distinction to all men, and that command is repeated innumerable times in the Bible in many ways and with different words, which he illustrated with the aforesaid Hebrew phases.[25]

In other ways Renan was contradictory. He praised Jews and showed the significant contributions of Judaism to the development of Christianity, but he persisted in prejudice because of his ignorance of the Talmud. Renan assiduously insisted that Judaism was rigid, narrow, and had been superceded by Christian teaching.[26] In response to these allegations, Jewish critics proclaimed Renan's pen was dipped in "gall" and peppered with errors. Further, they attacked his descriptions of the condemnation of

Jesus, which Renan imputed to the Jews. "Renan has furnished no proof whatsoever for this accusation," said one writer.[27] Another impassioned journalist wrote: "No—a thousand times—no, the death of Jesus was not the crime of a nation, as Renan declared. It is Jews who have suffered. The Jews have at all times been the victims, but not the executioners. Your assertion, M. Renan, is more than a calumny—it is an absurdity." Further, the writer continued, "The truth is, that if Christianity has lasted eighteen centuries, it is because it is a piece of Judaism. . . . Judaism alone is imperishable because it is the religion of the spirit and the heart, and because it is the liberty of the soul. . . ."[28] Joseph Salvador, a French Jewish scholar of religion agreed with these criticisms, although his views on Judaism were certainly unorthodox. (He sought a "heavenly Jerusalem" and a universal culture that would be a synthesis of religions.)[29]

Even a few non-Jews questioned Renan's judgements about the Jews. One was Ernest Bersot in the *Journal des Débats* who noted that Jews did not differ much from the early Christians in moral teaching, but rather in the religious practices of circumcision, the dietary laws, and the interdiction of mixed marriages. Only the obedience to these laws kept Judaism a sect; it was Jesus who made it a universal religion, and that is the story that Renan reveals.[30] Another writer, Ernest Havet (a professor in College of France), complained that Renan had many harsh things to say of the Jews. "He will not even allow Judaism the honor to have produced Jesus . . . for Jesus never deserted Jewish teaching." He further said: "Of pure Judaism I will say in a word—it is the Jews who have taught the rest of the world these two great things: martyrdom and charity. More is not needed to give lie to the hate and derision of the crowd, but more to guarantee to these people a faithful and pious respect."[31]

Ironically, Renan was denied his position in the University because of the publication of his book. Immediately, public opinion, especially the liberals and their developing opposition, was agitated over what it felt was the lack of freedom of speech and thought. The government, obviously reluctant to tangle with the church, dodged the issue of human rights neatly by the following subterfuge. Officials claimed that Renan's dismissal was based on his right to teach "theology." Originally, his appointment was based on his scholarly attainment in languages or philology. He had published *The General History and Comparative System of the Semitic Languages,* and additionally, the *Study of the Greek Language of the Middle Ages.* Both books had been hailed critically. In 1851 he had served in the Imperial Library, and in 1860 he received support for study in

Palestine and Syria. On his return in 1862 he had been given the Chair of Hebrew, Chaldean and Syrian languages (semitic languages). His appointment, declared Rouland, was based exclusively on his philological research. He was not permitted to lecture on religion which was strictly the right of the theologian. Renan had, therefore, disobeyed the directive implied in his contract of employment and "propounded doctrines which were offensive to the Christian faith, and which might give rise to lamentable agitation."[32] To emphasize the official viewpoint and to allay suspicion of prejudice and abuse of freedom of thought, Solomon Munk, a Jew and an eminent Hebraic scholar, was awarded the Chair.[33]

The Renan controversy was indeed an exemplar of the Jewish position in France. On the one hand, Renan had broken with the older, more traditional forms of Christianity, and he did recognize some Jewish contributions to Christian civilization. In that sense he represented the newer, more open and sensitive society that was appearing in the more secular and liberal intellectual French environment. In direct contrast to the studious and objective attempt to delineate the origins of Christianity, he held fast to some of the more traditional myths and faulty translations which continued to form the basis and the emotional content of French antisemitism. So too, did the same paradox appear in French society. While Jews were generally accepted in all levels of achievement and society there were pockets of French life in which they still suffered either exclusion or denunciation such as, perhaps, by a private club,[34] by a defamatory series of articles in the Alsatian press,[35] or by inappropriate policy of subordinate bureaucrats. Such rulings occurred most frequently in the armed forces, where officers sometimes forced both Jewish and Protestant soldiers to attend Catholic services and fetes.[36] Protests by the Consistories sometimes brought relief when the Minister of Religion forbade such treatment.

Conclusion

The nature of French antisemitism that has been described in the foregoing chapters indicated that its roots were founded in the religious traditions and the developing political struggles arising from the new forces of nationalism and secularism. The antagonism toward Jews evolved from two sources: politics and religion, and neither was translated into violent action (except on rare occasions in Alsace). Racism was the one factor that was not present Yet, the most significant and persistent ideologue of racism that influenced modern European prejudice wrote extensively during this time. Arthur de Gobineau's important work on the inequality of races appeared in 1853.

Gobineau was a legitimist dedicated to defending the aspirations and the status of a nobility assailed by the challenges of modernity. He, as many others of his generation, regretted the decline of the older traditions and mourned the passing his class's hegemony. He regarded the French Revolution as an abomination and the French masses as a hotbed of mediocrity. Equality in the state leads, according to Gobineau, to social unrest and disorder. Despite the fact that his opinions, like that of the other ultramontanes, were reflective of the politics of resentment, he did not find his solutions in Catholic orthodoxy or even legitimacy. For him, the explanation of all social phenomenon rested upon the factor of race. Europe was fast degenerating morally and intellectually. The superior races were Caucasian: Celtic, and especially the Aryan-German, but these races had been contaminated by miscegenation. However, in his works Jews were not singled out as an inferior race, although they were part of the Semitic enemies which weakened the Aryans; they were not important in the subsequent downfall of European society. Indeed, he expressed some admiration for the accomplishment of the Jews. ". . . They became a people that succeeded in everything they undertook, a free, strong, and intelligent people, and one which, before they lost their status as an independent nation, had given us as many learned men to the world as it had merchants."[38]

Gobineau's main specter of doom for the world rested upon the Slavs, the Mongols and the Latins in general, of which Jews were only a small part. Although, the antisemitic sentiments expressed in this book and later works were critical of the modern Jews they represented the conventional anti-Jewish attitudes of his time. Indeed, he often displayed a respect for contemporary Jews: Jews were a population (in Alsace-Lorraine) of excellent worth, irreplaceable in her banks, her workshops, and her army."[39] The main force of Gobineau's influence, however, neither occurred in his time, nor in France. His ideas were not read widely in France (despite a second edition of his book in 1884), but they were disseminated through the influence of Wagner and Scheimann in Germany when the first Gobineau clubs were founded in 1894.[40] Even Charles Drumont, who used racist arguments in his vicious attacks upon Jews, never referred to Gobineau for his main premises.[41] Gobineau's works were not well received because in essence they were not reflective of the main currents of French thought. Social Darwinism was not an important element in French thought either. French attitudes were rather focused on ethnocentrism. They perceived French culture, language, and intellectual development as the mainspring of European civilization, and race per se had no real importance. Gobineau's works also were not in tune with the ultramontanes and the Legitimists who were seeking to defend Catholic orthodoxy and Papal power. [42]

The political roots of antisemitism which took shape during the Second Empire rested in the historical legacy of 1789. The French Revolution had created profound divisions in French society because it had established new institutions, deriving their legitimacy from the rational ideals of the Enlightenment. The major premise of the revolutionary zealots was the notion of liberty. That virtue emphasized individualism and the supremacy of one's own conscience. Moral behavior and ethical values, therefore, were determined by the individual because God had granted free will to make the proper ethical choices and to behave appropriately in the maintenance of justice. Therefore, the revolutionary state and its church established minimal limitations on people's lives. Their major role was to grant individuals as much freedom as they desired—so long as they did not harm others. The consequences of this freedom meant the acceptance of laissez faire economics, the removal of social and caste barriers, and the triumph of free competition. Jews and Protestants both benefited from these precepts, especially in business and education. The liberals also supported the notion of a sharp distinction between civil and religious affairs. Both the extreme right and the extreme left rejected this revolutionary heritage, and in the process Jews and Protestants were excoriated because *they* had accepted it.

The socialists denounced the individualism extolled by the revolution because they claimed it avoided the problems of poverty and exploitation. Free competition only exacerbated class divisions and reinforced bourgeois capitalist domination. Cooperation was their keystone to a better society. Jews became identifiable as financial lords, as the socialists called them. They described the yoke of feudal nobility as having shifted to new masters, the capitalists, the bankers, and the financiers. They referred often to the Rothschilds, Perieres, and the Foulds,[43] as has been noted. Scandals which involved Mirès, and the Credit mobilier associated with the Perieres, provided additional portraits for the scurrilous identification of "juif" with the unscrupulous capitalist. Jews were further stigmatized by their communal adherence to liberal principles and the prominence of Goodchaux and Crémieux in liberal politics verified socialist assumptions.[44]   As previously described, socialist rivalries added fuel to their dislike because Jews were prominent among the Saint Simonians.

However, socialist rhetoric played a small role in antisemitism during the Second Empire for the most prominent socialist writers were banned and their press was muzzled. Even a Jewish socialist, Armand Levy, long friendly to the emperor, was denied the right to publish a paper.[45] Georges Duchêne, the most notable of the socialist publicists, did not enjoy a large audience, and his political influence did not become a major force until after 1870.[46] Socialist rhetoric from its onset during the Revolution of 1848 remained ideological and political. Jews were a good scapegoat to polarize their basically anti-bourgeois, anti-capitalist bias. In addition, many socialists were also anti-religious in general, and thus attacked Judaism in order to obliquely criticize Christianity.[47] Interestingly, after the Dreyfus Affair the identification of the extreme conservatives with antisemitism caused some socialists to abandon their attacks upon the Jews.[48]

Thus socialist antisemitism was combined with a vision of a different society. Proudhon was essentially anti-modern and despised the new entrepreneurs and the "cash nexus" of the developing modern state. As indicated earlier, Toussenel alone maintained more religious biases. Later, radical socialists or anarchists such as Blanqui, Proudhon, and Duchêne became equally anti-republican, after the downfall of the empire. Subsequently, some of their adherents supported the nationalist Catholic conservatives in their antagonism towards Jews during the Dreyfus Affair.[49]

However, the most vociferous and conspicuous antisemitism was expressed by the extreme right during the Second Empire, and its influence was more profound and enduring. The mainspring of their negativism derived from religious inspiration. They, too, opposed the libertarian and individualistic tenets of the Revolution, but in contrast to the socialists they claimed that the revolutionary constitution protected the enemies of God and his servants. The tenuous alliance between Bonaparte and the church also provided more opportunity for clerical writers to propagate their views. The government tended to be more circumspect in suppressing their press and literature because many of hierarchy, and even the Pope himself, supported these views. In reality, the ultramontanes were a militant minority and their papers enjoyed a very small circulation. However, few expressed anger or dismay over this vicious antisemitism; rather the prevailing sentiment was apathy or passivity. One of the reasons was certainly that some influential Catholics surreptitiously supported the ultramontanes, but also, there prevailed widespread and longstanding misconceptions of Judaism inherited from the middle ages.[50] Since the Holocaust many religious writers have debated the Christian origins of antisemitism. One theologian, Rosemary Ruether, suggested that the anti-Jewish passages in the New Testament and the patristic fathers was the result of a bitter competition by Christians in their drive to overtake Judaism.[51] Another writer declared that the central conception of Christianity, the crucifixion, was dependent upon the myth that Jews played a major role in the death of Jesus (the scapegoat for human sins) and hence became the pariah people central to Christian belief.[52] Whatever the source, this religious antisemitism was a part of the general mentality of nineteenth century France.

These prevailing beliefs rested upon the perception of Judaism only as a precursor of Christianity which, in turn, was the ultimate fulfillment of the covenant. Jewish degradation and suffering in exile was not only punishment for sin, but also was a part of the curse Jews endured because they had rejected the true messiah. The only way they could gain salvation and forgiveness was to accept the Roman Catholic religion. Furthermore, Judaism was rigid and static, basing its tenets on legalistic, dry formulas. In contrast, Christianity was based on love and a higher spirituality. Since the Jews killed Jesus, they were punished by being forced to live in the diaspora. Catholics, convinced that there could be no salvation outside of the Church, believed that missionary activity was an inherent good. Most Christians regarded Judaism as an archaic religion; the Talmud and the Mishna represented not a developing theology and civilization, but rather a backward, formal, and erroneous body of doctrine. These perceptions were commonly held by all levels of society. Such notions are still common, even in our time, as evidenced by Toynbee's characterization of Judaism as a "fossilized religion."[53] The ultramontanes fiercely asserted these doctrines, but liberal Catholics, too, never understood the tenets of the Jewish faith, and accepted without question this teaching of the church. The two most eloquent examples of this myopia were in the contrasting works of DeBonald and Lamennais.

DeBonald was a legitimist conservative. Jews, for him, could not be or become French unless they converted. Religious freedom was unthinkable. On the other hand, Lamennais had accepted the revolution and sought to reconcile the Roman Catholic Church with the exigencies of modernization. Nevertheless, he, too, repeated those same accusations which were an integral part of the Catholic tradition. He accused Jews of bearing the sign of Cain, and he used the term "deicide" to describe their role in the crucifixion. He saw Jews as a part of the hated "Pharisees," and the Talmud as a symbol of their blindness.[54]

These ideas were often reflected in sermons, teachings, and the general works of the time.[55] The official church attitude which cultivated these notions remained unchanging during the Second Empire. The Catholic ideal was that all Jews should sooner or later become Catholic, hence religious antisemitism was fully *legitimized* by the church. Protestants' ideas about Jews were similar, but as a minority, they were more sympathetic to the precepts of 1789. They refrained from open criticism of the Jews, although they, too, were ardent evangelicals.

This form of religious antisemitism or misinformation was encountered almost everywhere in daily life. One example of such insensitivity occurred in 1861. In the trial of Abbé Mallet the prosecutor, in defending Jewish family rights and excoriating excessive proselytization, characterized Sarah Bluth as a fine woman, "although in religious error," and later in the trial he declared that conversion was an ultimate good. Protests of the Jewish consistories, which pointed out that freedom of religion meant recognition of each faith's legitimacy, caused the prosecutor to apologize.[56]

These sentiments were often repeated in the works of philo-semites and liberal writers. Crémieux wrote a letter on 17 February 1865 to *Opinion Nationale*, criticizing the preface to *Julius Caesar* by Napoleon III, for referring to the fact that Jews had crucified "their messiah."[57] In the same vein, Rabbi Isador wrote to Victor Duruy about his *History of France* indicating that the former had written a derogatory phrase about Jews. Duruy responded by writing an apologetic letter, promising to delete the offending sentence.[58] Even the most learned and liberal scholars were thus committed to the proposition that eventually Jews would convert; that outside the church there would be no salvation; and that the full moral development of the Jew could only occur by his acceptance of Christ. Such an attitude was enunciated in an article by Abbé Michaud in *Correspondant* (25 December 1867), a paper that represented the liberal Catholic viewpoint. The article was friendly to Jews, and the author revealed an unusual knowledge of Judaism and the Jewish community; yet Michaud could not abandon his tradition. He ended his comments by saying: "It was through Christianity that the principles of Judaism became spiritual and universal."[59]

The debates and protests by Jewish journalists to what they considered derogatory or patronizing statements about Judaism neither reflected a heightened sensitivity or nit-picking critiques. Jews had developed in the diaspora a highly sophisticated and evolving religious theology. Despite the paucity of Franco-Jewish scholarship, that community was aware and proud of their spiritual heritage and its subsequent development throughout Europe. Moreover, they believed in the revolutionary principle of religious freedom, but that tradition had a different significance for the Jews than it did for Catholics. For Jews, it meant acceptance of their religious values, traditions, and theology as being equally moral and legitimate as Christianity. On the other hand, freedom for most Frenchmen meant *toleration* or restraint from open persecution. For them, emancipation meant assimilation and perhaps eventual absorption of the Jewish community. In the nineteenth century few Christians perceived Judaism as a separate valid ethical tradition, and they were insensitive to its continuous vitality. Jews were seen at best as assimilated Frenchmen, at worst as aliens or foreigners. Thus missionary activity, lauded as a positive good, only offended Jews who perceived it as an ongoing threat to their survival, and an assault on their beliefs.

Despite the unanimity over the superiority of its beliefs, the church, too, was torn by disagreements. Catholic liberals espoused the universal principles of liberty and suggested that the Church must reconcile itself to these ideals and support freedom of conscience and the scientific spirit engendered by industrialization. They had been inspired by Bishops such as Montalembert and Dupanloup, and the teachings of Lamennais and Lacordaire. Lamennais' paper, *Avenir,* had in 1830-31 first enunciated principles such as separation of church and state, freedom for all religious thought, schools freed from the influence of the centralized state authority of the University, liberty of press and association, and the decentralization of government power. However, these ideas were too liberal for acceptance by the Papacy and they were condemned. As good Catholics Montalembert, Lacordaire, and Lamennais submitted to the authority of the Church, and desisted in writing openly in defense of those liberties which they had so passionately advocated. Lamennais later left the church to reassume support of his more modern visions. Montalembert and Lacordaire remained loyal to the Papacy, but they did not become ultramontanes.[60] Indeed, Montalembert continued to defend the ideal of the French Revolution in a more moderate manner and soon became one of the spokesmen for the liberal Catholics during the Second Empire. He advocated Gallican ideas and supported religious toleration. Bishop Dupanloup, on the other hand, eager to compromise with modernity, never reconciled himself to either liberty of worship or the press.[61]

Conservatives affirmed their belief that there was only one path to salvation, and hence, no compromise could be permitted with truth.

These ultramontane Catholics also supported the absolute moral supremacy of the Pope and allied themselves with the Legitimists (partly in reaction to the Emperor's Roman policy and growing liberalism). They demanded that the state maintain the essential moral values of the Catholic Church. They declared that man was conceived in original sin and salvation was obtained only through the Church. Therefore, they shared the conservative view that man was essentially evil and would remain so as long as he was alienated from God. In their eyes, the only way to achieve social amelioration and progress would be through obedience to the teachings of the Church.

Hence, in the eyes of the ultramontanes, the Revolution of 1789 was a disaster because it ruptured the necessary alliance between the throne and the altar. This disruption weakened French society by attenuating traditional values and sapping the respect that cemented social relationships. Just as the socialists deplored the evils of individualism, so did the ultramontanes.

For the latter, the revolution had exalted science and secularism, the twin evils of modernism, as explicated in the Syllabus of Error in 1864. The Catholic Church alone was the source of truth, and the state's function was to impose and implement these truths in all of its institutions. Society, the ultramontanes and their legitimist allies claimed, should perpetuate and emphasize respect for religion, family and property. While conservatives correctly perceived that restoration of the ancien regime was impossible, they hoped only to preserve the best features of the past. The state's duties should include the denial of individualism promulgated by the revolution and the restoration of religious fidelity, holiness, charity, probity, hard work and discipline. Religious freedom was anathema to them because there was only one morality, and fidelity to Catholic tradition was the strongest barrier to social upheaval. Individual rights, therefore, were always subordinate to the demands and loyalties of the hierarchy and to the authority of the family and adherence to tradition.[62]

On the other hand, liberal Catholics abandoned many of these precepts. They supported the notion of a "Gallican" church, while maintaining their support for the Pope's temporal power. They endeavored to reconcile Catholic principles with revolutionary ideals. Some supported freedom of religion and the press, and some were even sympathetic to nationalism.[63] As devoted to the church as their more conservative brethren, and just as convinced in their faith, they were more open to modern thought and more tolerant of others' faiths. Yet in the Dupanloup tradition, many liberal Catholics devoted to the Church's interests desired a liberal Catholic state. Hence, there was a marked divergence between the Catholic clergy's responses to the Mortara affair and behavior in the Mallet and the Linneweil Affairs.

In public life, too, there were some notable examples of good will toward Jews. The Archbishop of Paris, at a meeting of the Imperial Council of public instruction, conceded that charity, "one of the essential principles of the Christian religion," was a Jewish virtue long before it became a Christian one. He went on to demand that the state had the obligation to guarantee the liberty of conscience for everyone.[64] The anti-clerical *Siècle*, in a rare moment, lauded the public Catholic appreciation of the appeals of Crémieux and various rabbis on behalf of Syrian Christians.[65]

Thus, throughout the nineteenth century and even into the twentieth century, French society heatedly debated church-state relationships, and the nature and structure of the state's institutions. These conflicts permeated discussions of foreign policy, family rights, individual rights, and education. Unfortunately, as already demonstrated, Jewish issues were frequently interjected into these debates, and gradually the rhetoric of antisemitism which had been essentially religious, became politicized.

This climate of opinion was abetted by a variety of clerical writers and their legitimist allies. The most important of these polemicists were David (Paul) Drach, Theodore Ratisbonne, Louis Veuillot, and Gougenot de Mousseaux. Drach and Ratisbonne were Jewish converts to Catholicism and their arguments were more religiously antagonistic than the latter two.[66]

Drach was especially eager to convert his fellow Jews.[67] To do so he resorted to arguments which were typical of the nineteenth century missionary. Since Jesus himself was Jewish, his teachings evolved out of that tradition, and Drach and others refrained from denouncing the Mosaic law. The Talmud, developing later, was the target by which they tried to demolish Jewish learning. Hence, Drach claimed the religion of the ancient Hebrews was identical to Catholicism and the many ceremonies and practices of the church were still extant in the synagogue. He insisted that the rituals of the Jews had become Pharisaical and that the Talmud was "the fruit of superstitious practices and reveries; it is a monstrous compilation, a true encyclopedia in which there is no good sense."[68] Only Catholicism could regenerate ancient verities because those have been overwhelmed by the Talmud whose "reasoning is so specious, so subtle, so grotesque, that it is difficult to understand."[69]   And he went even further in his invective by declaring: "Rabbinical cynicism revolts the Christian with its atrocities, calumnies, and impious hate that the Pharisees extend to all objects of religious veneration."[70]   These negative judgements were seized by later antisemites who quoted them extensively and used them to propagate their own hate.[71]

On the other hand, Theodore Ratisbonne, though more assimilated and worldly than Drach, became just as committed to his new faith. In his works, Theodore Ratisbonne castigated Jews claiming that they possessed the instincts of domination and that they invaded all the avenues which led to riches and power. Further, by denying Christ, Jews have been persecuted by all peoples as an integral part of God's punishment. The Catholics, he declared, had attempted to moderate this chastisement by even providing an asylum for Jews in the Ghetto. Ratisbonne repeated Drach's charge that Judaism was rigid and legalistic. He also associated the French Revolution of 1789 with Jewish development because the revolution exposed Jews to a "licentious society." Consequently, Jews were seduced by eighteenth century philosophy, and they embraced secularism. The result, he claimed, left many Jews no longer Jews, but not yet Christians. "They float in danger," said Ratisbonne, "caught between their past and the future."[72]

The works of Drach and Ratisbonne were neither original, scholarly, nor theologically significant. Their Hebrew translations were frequently faulty and their interpretations of scripture would have been vehemently derided by them *before* their conversion.[73] Their importance derived from their influence upon the thought of Veuillot and Gougenot des Mousseaux. Both of these writers, especially Mousseaux, drew heavily upon them, for they were considered exemplary Hebrew scholars and as ex-Jews their works were presumed to possess more validity. Thus, Veuillot and Mousseaux's misconceptions were reinforced by their conviction that they had consulted Jewish authorities.

Unfortunately, neither Veuillot nor Mousseaux possessed the perspicacity to question or test either the scholarship or the psychological mainsprings of Drach's and Ratisbonne's works; for the ultramontanes wished the affirmation of their own beliefs. In truth, Drach and Ratisbonne reflected the ambiguities and self hate which plagued their conversion.[74]

Religious conversion involved a momentous shift in identity, loyalty, and values. It meant that Drach and the Ratibonne brothers suffered a considerable discontinuity in their behavior and thought. They had to reconstruct their personalities, verbal imagery, memories, and motives in order to match their newly adopted system of values and rationalizations. Whatever their special psychological motives for conversion,[75] both subjects were also obsessed by a desire to cross the insuperable boundary between the majority group and their minority status in order to achieve full acceptance. This made them what Lewin characterized as "marginal men" creating a social psychological phenomenon in which self doubts were transformed into Jewish self hate.[76] By denying their own past and their families and seeking acceptance by the adopted group, the apostates resolved their cognitive dissonance by rejecting the vocabulary and beliefs of their own heritage. They chose the newer values which included the majority's perceptions of their own people. Both converts "internalized" the negative stereotypes held by the majority group.[77] Both men became fervent missionaries, aggressively carrying their message to fellow Jews, seeking to mitigate their own conflicts. Not all converts were afflicted with self-hate. Many did use religious conversion as a way of solving deeply held psychological or social needs. Achille Fould supposedly converted to Protestantism, yet maintained his ties with the Jewish community. Father Jacob Libermann (converted by Drach) became a missionary to the Blacks. He felt irritated by what he called the excessive "manipulation" in the conversion of Jews. He refused to denigrate Judaism and urged prudence and discretion toward his fellow Jews.[78] Louis Veuillot and Gougenot des Mousseaux, devout (almost fanatical in their devotion), sought evidence that would buttress their campaign against Judaism, secularism, and Protestantism. They found it in the passionate imagery of Drach's and Ratisbonne's self hate. These writers were the precursors of modern French antisemitism.

Louis Veuillot, who leaned heavily on the works of Drach and Charini in his denunciation of the Talmud, was also the passionate advocate of the Papal cause; totally uncritical of church policy and its history. The inquisition, condemned by liberals and regretted by most Catholics, was ardently defended by Veuillot. He perpetuated the tradition of religious antisemitism and helped to politicize it. In 1870 Veuillot wrote these words which foreshadowed later nationalistic sentiments of the conservative Catholics:

As a French Christian Catholic, rooted in France like
ancient oak trees, I am made, unmade, governed,
ruled, shaped by vagabonds in culture and tradition. Renegades or aliens, they (Jews) share neither
my faith, nor my prayers, nor my memories, nor
my fears. I am subjected to the heretic, to the Jew,
to the atheist—to those who are of a nature which
most resembles the brute.[78]

L'Univers, Veuillot's paper, appealed to many of the clergy and the
bishops. Often they prevented the more moderate elements in the church
from silencing or even controlling this religious fanaticism. To add to his
credibility, Veuillot enjoyed the approbation of the Papacy itself (despite
some misgivings over his methods).[79] Veuillot was far better known and
influential during the Second Empire than Gougenot des Mousseaux, yet in
the long run, he had less significance on the subsequent development of
hate. In contrast, Gougenot des Mousseaux's book, published in 1869,
hardly caused a ripple in the publishing business. Nevertheless, Norman
Cohn credited Mousseaux's work as being the "Bible of modern antisemitism."[80]

Gougenot des Mousseaux, aristocrat and legitimist, was born 22
April 1805 in Coulommiers (Seine et Marne). He was a devout Catholic
who served as "gentleman of chamber," at the court of King Charles X. He
retired to his chateau at Coulommiers after the revolution of 1830, where
he served on the Municipal Council. He devoted the rest of his life to the
study of magic, primitive religion, satanism, and the Jews. Gradually he
became convinced that Jews were evil and dangerous. He died on 5 October 1876. His most nefarious work was entitled *The Jew, Judaism, and the
Judaization of the Christian Peoples*. The book's major premises were that
Jews were thinkers who merged the rational philosophies of the eighteenth
century enlightenment with the conspiratorial weapons of Free Masonry,
to plan and eventually dominate the world and Christianity. He cited
Drach and Ratisbonne extensively in his analytical attack upon the Talmud.
He, too, repeated the canards that the Talmud was pernicious, evil, and
immoral, and as other Catholic writers had claimed, Mousseaux argued
that the Talmud had replaced the Mosaic law. Further, he insisted that
Jewish money controlled the world press and thus had developed the secularization of Europe. He asserted that the Catholic Austrian defeat by
Protestant Prussia was living proof of the Jewish plot. He, like many

other Catholics, condemned emancipation, not only because he detested religious freedom, but also because Jews were aided by government subsidies for their synagogues. He insisted that the Jews had allied themselves with Satan, and his magic was revealed in their study of the Kabbala. Hence he defended Roumanian antisemitism by declaring that it was the result of evil Jewish practices. On the whole, the book was verbose, illogical, unknowledgeable, and the scholarly sources cited were very questionable.[81] Though the book sold poorly in France, it was published in Austria and Roumania in 1876. Poor sales, however, did not preclude its good press reviews which appeared in many Catholic books and papers, including *Le Monde*.[83] That paper praised the book for informing everyone about the prevailing dangers to Christian society. *Le Monde* continued:

> The revolution has entered into Judaism, and has fed its implacable hate of Christianity. . . . This hate of Christianity, which is a tradition of Judaism, far from being enfeebled by the indifference of modernism, has been fortified by these Revolutionary principles which, in turn, has directed its fury against Catholicism; religious liberty, therefore, is an insult and becomes a menace for the existence of Christianity.[82]

Gougenot's work represented, as the reviews indicated, Christian resentment of Jews and was reflective of ultramontane and legitimist prejudices. He was not interested in public opinion or political power. His ideas might have passed unnoticed, but unfortunately Edward Drumont a far more influential anti-semite later on, found the book useful and revived it. In 1886 he encouraged the Mousseaux family to finance another edition. This time the book, promoted by Drumont himself, enjoyed a wider audience. The preface was written by Father Voisin, head of the Paris Foreign Mission Seminary, and even more damaging was the fact that the book had the blessing of Pius IX who commended Mousseaux for his courageous views.[83] The delineation of the "satanic" Jew by Veuillot and Mousseaux psychologically conditioned some French Catholics for the racist conspiratorial rhetoric of Drumont. Drumont used Mousseaux's ideas and grafted his racist dogma to the traditional theological antagonisms. As France became even more secularized, the next step was Charles Maurras, who used Catholic antagonisms toward the revolution to attack the despised republic, and then turned against the church itself.

Moreover, Mousseaux had revived the medieval conception of the Jews as agents of Satan, whose mission was to tempt Christians into eternal damnation.[84] This imagery made possible the virulence of later antisemitism, for the ultramontanes disliked Protestants and Freemasons as vehemently as they did Jews. Protestants suffered hostility frequently from government officials, the established church, and the general populace. The conflicts were bitterly criticized in the English press, and arose primarily because missionary societies (both Anglican and Methodist) engaged in very aggressive proselytization which was bitterly resented by the Church. Overzealous government officials often equated such preaching with revolutionary movements.[85] Yet despite the antagonisms between these faiths, Catholic and Protestant rhetoric was never marked by the same slanders or the venomous animosity evidenced against the Jews, because tradition had not provided the scurrilous dialogue as it had for the Jews.

As already indicated in earlier chapters, the debates and passionate rhetoric of the Roman Question involved conflicts over the direction of French society. What was even more significant was that as the legitimists and Catholics sought to retrieve former privileges, they also reflected fear and anger at the increasing pace of change. Just as the socialists and anarchists excoriated the new entrepreneur and emerging financial capitalist, the right feared the moral and political consequences of modernization. The moral underpinnings of their world were shaken, just as their hierarchic values and status were eroded. Antisemitism offered both the *right* and the *left* an acceptable vocabulary by which they could attack the perceived evils of their world.[87]

Nevertheless, in spite of all the existing negative factors extant during this period, relationships between Christians and Jews were very good on the whole between 1850 and 1878. The circumstances that created such a benign environment were found in the following factors: The period was one of relative peace and prosperity, and social conflicts were minimal and largely repressed. The government itself was determined to uphold the principles of religious liberty. The policies (already discussed) were aided by repression. The paradox of the Empire was that in order to promote freedom of conscience, it was necessary to deny freedom of the press. By preventing the widespread dissemination of hate literature the government sought to minimize factors of antisemitism. During the Third

Republic, freedom meant that Drumont could publish *freely* and appeal to the disaffected without risk. *Le France juive* probably could not have been published earlier.

The widespread secularization of French life led to passivity and indifference to both religious teaching and preaching. Parents demanded moral training in the primary schools because they wished to ensure the status quo, and maintain social stability. They were not interested in religious theology or practice. Hence they remained relatively indifferent to the issues of the temporal power, and openly sympathized with the Mortara and Coen parents. The indifference to religious issues attenuated the effect of antisemitism, which had been legitimized by traditional Catholic teaching.

Even the factor of French xenophobia was minimized in this period. Jews, always perceived as the "outsiders" because of their peculiar ethnic and religious culture, assimilated rapidly into French life. France, since 1789, had been the traditional refuge, the country of political asylum. Jewish immigration was not politically inspired, but those oppressed in Eastern Europe always saw France as a source of hope. Jews emigrated to France regularly and continuously.[86] However, in the years between 1850 and 1878, the numbers were small and although the migrants tried to continue their older tradition,[87] they were not very visible.

The "Napoleonic" bargain was observed by both sides. Jews abandoned Yiddish and preserved their French identity (even the Alliance Israelite Universelle perpetuated French culture and language in its schools in Palestine and North Africa). On the other hand, French government and society maintained few barriers to total Jewish absorption. Since racism was never an issue in French life, intermarriage was frequent, and often (if the dowry was large enough), quite acceptable. Napoleon III, the Empress Eugenie, Prince Napoleon, and indeed, the French society, accepted Jews socially.[88] There were legitimists and others who might disdain dialogue and treat Jews with contempt, but acceptance at the highest levels made such snobbery less overt or prevalent.

French antisemitism, then, was a minor force in French life, only reactivated by the trauma of military defeat, and social and political crises. The Franco-Prussian War altered immigration patterns which, in turn, heightened Jewish visibility. There was, in 1870, a large influx of Alsatian Jews into Paris, which was followed later with a steady stream of Polish and Russian Jews. These Eastern European Jews did not choose to accept the "Napoleonic" bargain as readily as their French confreres. Xenophobia exacerbated by defeat was given an impetus by the influx of Eastern European Jews who maintained their ethnic identity and culture. Antisemitism, consequently, flourished viciously and dangerously in the Dreyfus Affair, in the great depression, and in the Vichy regime: all periods of acute anxiety and despair.

The nature of French antisemitism, predicated upon long tradition and history, revealed ambiguities in all groups. It was the product of French social pathology that revealed the contradictions inherent in French society: liberalism coupled with social conservatism, ethnocentrism with cosmopolitanism, asylum and xenophobia. As Lewin so cogently noted:

> How little relation exists between Jewish conduct and antisemitism is well illustrated by the way the majority shifts its official reasons for maltreatment. For hundreds of years the Jews have been persecuted for religious reasons. Today racial theories serve as pretext. The reasons are easily changed according to whatever seems to be the most efficient argument at the moment. . . .[89]

The trauma of the Franco-Prussian War had psychologically damaged French attitudes about the nation and its culture. The national consciousness had been shocked and disrupted by defeat, occupation, and the Commune. These disturbances and a continuing modernization increased xenophobia and sharpened class conflicts. Many began to seek other values and moralities and different spiritual meanings. Hence there developed (especially among the young), the growth of patriotism and the desire for a new anti-rational esprit or elan. The right had always accepted such a posture: it had claimed to represent the real French truths: church, army, family and tradition. They claimed the denial of these traditions brought national punishment. Only a return to the folds of the Holy Church and the state, which had always been her eldest daughter, could bring remediation, claimed the conservatives.

At hand were the works of Gougenot des Mousseaux, rewritten and reshaped by Drumont, who substituted racial and national themes for the older religious animosities. The legitimacy which theological antisemitism had long enjoyed became attached to the new political strains introduced by Drumont and then Maurras. Assumptionist fathers, and others felt no moral compunctions in accepting these books and articles as the

Jew had been cursed by God and was morally inferior. It was not difficult to transfer older perceptions into the new dialogue with ease. That factor more than any other made Drumont's invective acceptable to many essentially decent conservatives. It was this factor that long preserved the antisemitic tradition in French life, a subterranean one, perhaps, but viable, enduring, and dangerous. Though largely invisible and imperceptible, this tradition lay hidden and seemingly inert. However, in periods of crisis and social upheaval, this ugly theme of antisemitism reappeared, as in World War II, and gave rise to abandonment, insensitivity, moral obtuseness, and at worst, collaboration in genocide.

[1] David Landes, "Religion and Enterprise: The Case of the French Textile Industry," in Edward C. Carter II; Robert Forster, and Joseph N. Moody, (eds.), *Enterprise and Entrepreneurs in Nineteenth-Century and Twentieth-Century France*, (Baltimore & London: John Hopkins Univ. Press, 1974), 68-70.

[2] *Jewish Chronicle*, (London), 22 November 1867.

[3] Echard, 245; Girard, 245-90; *Archives Israélites*, September 1867.

[4] c.f. J. L. Talmon, "Social Prophetism in Nineteenth-Century France. The Jewish Element in the Saint-Simonian Movement," *Commentary*, 26 (Aug. 1958): 158-72.

[5] *Times*, (London), 17 December 1862; *Jewish Chronicle*, (London), 20 December 1862; Fritz Stern, *Gold and Iron*, (New York: Knopf, 1977), 172-73; Cohen, *Promotion des juifs*, II, 476-77.

[6] For more analysis of the Rothschilds and Pereires, and banking in general, c. f. Anka Muhlstein, *The Rise of the French Rothschilds*, (New York & Paris: Vendome, 1983).

[7] Barrie M. Ratcliffe, "Some Jewish Problems in the Early Careers of Emile and Isaac Pereire," *Jewish Social Studies*, 34 (1972): 201.

[8] *Jewish Chronicle*, (London), 13 January 1870.

[9] P. de Rivoire d'Heilly, "Une élection exemplaire sous le Second Empire," *Revue Administrative*, 174 (1976): 681-83.

[10] Richard Terdiman, *Discourse, Counter Discourse*, (Ithaca: Cornell Univ. Press, 1985).

[11] See pp. 58.

[12] J. Morienal, *Les créateurs de la grande presse en France: Emile de Girardin, H. de Villemessant, Moïse Millaud*, (Paris: Alcan, 1934); Cohen, *La Promotion des juifs*, II, 484-87; Roger Bellet, *Le presse et journalisme*, (Paris, 1967) 119-125; Echard, 396-97.

[13] Cohen, *La Promotion des juifs*, II, 488-89.

[14] Ibid.

15 c. f. Letter to the editor, January 1867, *Archives Israélites,* related an episode in which a Jewish student was teased by his Catholic schoolmates. The father petitioned the Minister of Education for protection. The Minister criticized the college administrator. The latter apologized to the father for not protecting the boy. *Jewish Chronicle,* (London), 1 February 1867.

16 Hippolyte Castille, *Les Frères Péreires,* (Paris, 1861).

17 David Landes, "French Entrepreneurs and Industrial Growth in the Nineteenth Century," *Journal of Economic History,* 9 (May 1949): 45-49.

18 *Jewish Chronicle,* (London), 10 August 1865; Cohen, *Promotion des Juifs,* II, 650.

19 Ernest Feydeau, *Mémoire d'un coulissier,* (Paris, 1873).

20 J. P. Capefugue, *Histoire des grands opérations financières,* (Paris, 1855-60).

21 Edouard Drumont, *La France juive, essai d'histoire contemporaine,* (Paris,1886); c. f. Ratcliffe, "Jewish Problems in the Careers of the Pereires," 201.

22 Renan, *Life of Jesus,* (New York: Modern Library, Random House, 1927, 1955), 357-60, 382. It should be noted that in later works Renan expressed some denigration of the semites and their contribution to civilization. However, Renan uses racial terms in referring to culture and language, as well as to inherited traits. His racism is confusing. c. f. Pierre Guiral, "Renan et Maurras," *Etudes Maurrassiennes,* 1 (1972): 71-80; Léon Poliakov, *The Aryan Myth,* translated by Edmund Howard (New York: Meridian Book), 1971, 201-03.

23 Ibid.

24 *Jewish Chronicle,* (London), 11 September 1863.

25 *Archives Israélites,* August 1863

26 Renan, *Vie de Jesus.*

27 *Archives Israélites,* August 1863.

28 Ibid.

29 *Jewish Chronicle,* (London), 2 September 1864; Cohen, *La Promotion des juifs,* II, 737-39; *Encyclopedia Judaica,* 14, 716-717.

30 Cohen, *La promotion des juifs,* II, 737; *Archives Israélites,* Oct. 1864.

31 Ernest Havet, *Revue de deux Mondes,* 46 (1 August 1863): 592-95. Adolph Crémieux wrote a letter of thanks to that journal, and concluded by saying: "I regret (Renan's) objectionable opinions."

32 *Times,* (London), 20 June 1863; c. f. *Jewish Chronicle,* (London), 2 September 1864.

33 Ibid.

34 *Jewish Chronicle,* (London), 10 April 1857.

35 Ibid., 23 July 1869.

36 Complaints of Consistories, AN, F 19, 10129; *Times,* (London), 23 July 1864.

37 Ibid.

38 Arthur de Gobineau, *Essai sur l'inégalité des races humaines,* (Paris: Pierre Belfond, 1967), 85.

39 Michael D. Bidiss, *Father of Racist Ideology: The Social and Political Thought of Count Gobineau*, (New York: Weybright and Talley, 1970), 254-55.

40 Linda Clark, *Social Darwinism in France*, (University, Ala.: University of Alabama Press, 1984): 148-51.

41 Frederick Busi, *The Pope of Antisemitism: The Career and Legacy of Edouard-Adolphe Drumont*, (Lanham, New York, London: University Press of America, 1986), 60.

42 c. f. Clark, 150-71.

43 Victor M. Glasberg, "Intent and Consequences: The Jewish Question," *Jewish Social Studies*, 36 (Jan. 1974): 61-71.

44 Crémieux had remained politically active and ran as an opposition candidate in the elections for the Legislative Body in 1863. George Lichtheim, "Socialism and the Jews," *Dissent*, 15 (July-Aug. 1968): 314-42.

45 Police Report, 1 July 1861, AN F 18, 281; Isser, *Second Empire and the Press*, 5.

46 Lichtheim, "Socialism and the Jews," 314-42.

47 c. f. Edmund Silberner, "French Socialism and the Jewish Question, 1865-1914,"*Historia Judaica*, 15 (April 1954): 3-38.

48 Robert L. Hoffman, *More Than a Trial, the Struggle over Captain Dreyfus*, (New York: Free Press, 1980): 70-86; 125-131.

49 Ibid.; Lichtheim, "Socialism and the Jews," 314-42.

50 Jeremy Cohen, *The Friars and the Jews*, (Ithaca, London: Cornell University Press, 1983); Norman Cohn, *Warrant for Genocide*, (New York: Harper Torchbook, 1969).

51 Rosemary Ruether, *Faith and Fraticide*; Edward Flannery, *Anguish of the Jews*.

52 Hyam Maccoby, "Theologian of the Holocaust," *Commentary*, 74 (Dec. 1982): 33-37.

53 Arnold Toynbee, *A Study of History*, (New York and London: Oxford Univ. Press, 1947), 8, 22, 135, 361, 380, 388-9, 509.

54 Katz, *From Prejudice to Destruction*, 115-16.

55 Marseille Israelite Consistory to Prefect, AN, F19, 11031; Weber, 39-40.

56 *Archives Israélites*, April, May 1861.

57 *L'Opinion Nationale*, 17 February 1865; *Jewish Chronicle*, (London), 10 March 1865; 21 April 1865.

58 *Jewish Chronicle*, (London), 16 March 1865.

59 Cohen, *La Promotion des juifs*, II, 708-14.

60 C. B. Hastings, "Hugues-Félicité Robert de Lamennais: A Catholic Pioneer of Religious Liberty," *Journal of Church and State*, 30 (Spring 1988): 328-33; Alec Vidler, *Prophecy and Prophecy*, (New York: Scribners, 1954).

61 Zeldin, II, 1004-05.

62 *Le Monde*, 8 October 1861 quotes extensively from R. P. Ramière, *L'église et la civilization moderne*, (Paris, 1861); c. f. Robert Locke, *Legitimists and the Politics of Moral Order in the Early Third Republic*, (Princeton, N. J.: Princeton Univ. Press, 1974), 49, 262-65.

63 c. f. Lecanuet, R. P. *Montalembert*, (Paris, 1905).

64 *Jewish Chronicle*, (London), 16 March 1865.

65 *Le Siècle*, 16 August 1860; *Jewish Chronicle*, (London), 16 January 1864.

66 see pp. 72.

67 Paul Klein, "Mauvais juif, mauvais chrétien," *Revue de la Pensée juive*, 7 (1951): 87-103; Zosa Szajkowski, "Simon Deutz: Traitor or French Patriot ?" *Jewish Social Studies*, 16 (1965): 53-67; Catrice, 757-58.

68 Paul David Drach, Lettre d'un rabbin converti aux israélites ses frères sur les motifs de sa conversion, (Paris, 1925), 12.

69 Ibid., 76.

70 Ibid., 123.

71 Ibid., 123.

72 Theodore Ratisbonne, *La question juive*, (Paris, 1868), 2-84; c. f. Ratisbonne, *Réponses aux questions d'un israélite de notre temps*, (Paris, 1878).

73 Isser and Schwartz, " Sudden Conversion," *Jewish Social Studies*, 45 (Winter, 1983): 17-30.

74 Isser and Schwartz, "Psychohistory and Conversion," in J. Atlas (ed.), *Psychology and History*, (New York: Psychohistory Press, 1986): 321-57.

75 Isser and Schwartz, "Charismatic Leadership," *Cultic Studies Journal*, 3 (Spring, Summer, 1986): 57-78.

76 Kurt Lewin, *Resolving Social Conflict*, (New York: Harper and Row, 1948), 137.

77 Miriam Lewin Papnek, "Psychological Aspects of Minority Group Membership," *Jewish Social Studies*, 36 (1974): 72-79; Isser and Schwartz, "Minority Self-Hate," *Journal of Psychology and Judaism*, 11 (1987): 181-95.

78 Catrice, 283; c. f. Pierre Blanchard, *Le Vénérable Libermann, 1802-1852*, (Paris: Desclée de Brouver, 1960).

79 Gurian, "Louis Veuillot," 411; see pp.45.

80 Cohn, *Warrant for Genocide*, 41.

81 Gougenot des Mousseaux, *Le juif, le Judaisme et la judaisation des peuples chrétiens*, (Paris, 1869).

82 *Bibliographie catholique*, 43 (Paris, 1870): 211-215; *Polybiblion, Revue Bibliographie universelle*, 5 (Paris,1870): 186-88; Byrnes, 114.

83 Mousseaux, *Les juifs*, c. f. Byrnes, 114; E. Lovsky, *Antisemitisme et mystère d'Israel*, (Paris: Michel, 1955); Cohn, *Warrant for Genocide*, 41-51; Katz, *From Prejudice*, 113-144; Catrice, 541-65.

84 Joshua Trachtenberg, *The Devil and the Jews*, (Cleveland, New York: Meridian Books, 1943).

85 Procureur Report, Haut Saône, AN, BB30, 373; Prefect Report, October 1858, AN,

Fic III, 6; Report to Minister of Interior, March 1857, AN, F 18, 423; *Archives Israélites,* March 1858.

86 Cohen, *La Promotion des juifs,* I, 94-110.

87 Report of permission for Polish synagogue. AN, F 19, 5864.

88 Cohen, *La promotion des juif,* II, 125-30; c.f. Fritz Stern, *Gold and Iron,* (New York: Knopf, 1977), 172-73.

89 Lewin, 148-49.

Bibliography

Archival Sources

Archives Nationales, Paris
    BB 30 Ministry of Justice
    F 19 Ministry of Cults
    F 18 Press
    F 21 Theater
    Prefect Reports Fic III
Archives Departmentales
    Bouche du Rhône, Police reports M 6
    Rhône, Police reports M 6
    Haut Marne, Pre-trial interrogation
    Nord
Archives des Consistoire Centrale Israélite (Paris)
Archives des Ministère des Affaires Étrangères, Paris
Public Record Office/Foreign Office, London
Haus, Hof und Staatarchives, Vienna
Newspapers
    Archives Israélites
    L'Univers Israélite
    Le Siècle
    Le Monde
    L'Opinion Nationale
    L'Univers
    Revue des deux Mondes
    La Vérité Israélite, 1860-61.
    La Voix des Clubs, 1848
    Père Duchêne, 1848
    L'Organisation du Travail, 1848
    Der Israelitischen Volklehrer (Frankfurt am Main)
    London *Jewish Chronicle*
    London *Times*
    Morning Herald, London
    Morning Advertiser, London

Printed Sources

About, Edmond. *Lettres d'un bon jeune homme à sa cousine Madeleine.* Paris, 1861.

About, Edmund. *La Question Romaine.* Brussels, 1859.

Adam, Juliette. *Mes premières armes littéraires et politiques.* Paris, 1904.

Assézat, Jules. *L'Affaire Mortara, le droit du père.* Paris, 1858.

Astruc, Aristide. *Les juifs et Louis Veuillot.* Paris, 1858.

Chiala, Luigi. *Carteggio politico di Michelangelo Castelli,* 4 Vols., Rome, 1890-91.

Il Carteggio Cavour-Nigra dal 1858 al 1861, 2 Vols., Bologna: A cura della R. commissione editrice, 1926-29.

Castille, Hippolyte. *Les Frères Péreires.* (Paris, 1861).

La censure dramatique. Paris, 1873.

La censure sous Napoleon III, rapports inédits in extenso, 1852 à 1860. Paris, 1892.

Coyne, J. Stirling. *The Woman in Red.* New York, 1864.

Delacouture, Abbé. *Le droit canon et le droit naturel dans l'Affaire Mortara.* Paris, 1858.

Delord, Taxtile. *Histoire du Second Empire.* 7 Vols. Paris, 1869.

Drach, David P. *Lettre d'un rabbin converti aux Israélites ses frères sur les motifs de sa conversion.* Paris, 1825.

Ernest Feydeau. *Mémoire d'un coulisser.* Paris, 1873.

Gobineau, Arthur de. *Essai sur l'inégalité des races humaines.* Paris, Pierre Belfond, 1967.

Goncourt, Jules and Edmond de. *Journals des Goncourt, mémoires de la vie littéraire.* 2 Vols. Paris, 1910-11.

Havet, Ernest, "L'Evangile et l'histoire," *Revue de des Mondes,* 46 (1 August 1863): 564-96.

Klein, S. *Judaism ou la vérité sur le Talmud.* Paris, 1859.

Leven, Narcisse. *Cinquante ans d'histoire.* Paris: Alcan, 1911.

Mérimée, Prosper. *Lettres à M. Panizzi 1850-1870.* 2 Vols. Paris, 1871.

Mirès, Jules. *Mes juges, ma vie et mes affaires.* Paris, 1861.

Montifiore, Mose and Lady. *Dairies.* Chicago, 1890.

Mori, Renato (ed.). *La Questione Romana 1861-1865.* 2 Vols. Florence: F. Le Monnier, 1963.

Mousseaux, Gougenot des. *Le juif, le judaisme et la judaisation des peuples chrétiens.* Paris, 1869.

Normanby, Lord. *Memoirs of a Year of Revolution.* 2 Vols. London, 1848.

Ratisbonne, Théodore-Marie. *Ratisbonne, fondateur de la société des prêtres et de congrégation des religieuses de Notre-Dame de Sion.* 2 Vols. Paris, 1903.

Ratisbonne, Théodore-Marie. *Réponses aux questions d'un Israélite de notre temps.* Paris, Brussels, 1878.

Ratisbonne, Théodore-Marie. *La question juive.* Paris, 1868.

Ratisbonne, Théodore-Marie. *Quelque mots sur l'Affaire de la family Bluth.* Paris, 1861.

Renan, Ernest. *Life of Jesus.* New York: Modern Library, Random House, 1927, 1955.

Rupert, Louis. *L'église et la synagogue.* Paris, 1859.

Séjour, Victor. *La tireuse des cartes.* Paris, 1859.

Veuillot, Eugène. *Louis Veuillot*, 9th edition, 3 Vols. Paris: Lethielleux 1904.

Veuillot, Louis. *Oeuvres complètes*, Paris: Lethielleux, 1925.

Weill, Alexandre. *Lettres fraternelles à Louis Veuillot.* Paris, 1858.

Zazi, A. *La politica estera del regno delle Due Sicilie.* Naples, 1940.

Secondary Works

Adler, Cyrus and Margolith, Aaron M. *With Firmness on the Right: American Diplomatic Action Affecting Jews, 1840-1945.* New York: American Jewish Committee, 1946.

Ages, Arnold. "Veuillot and the Talmud," *Jewish Quarterly Review*, 64 (January 1974): 229-60.

Ages, Arnold. *The Diaspora Dimension.* Hague: Nijhoff, 1973.

Agulhon, Maurice. *The Republican Experiment 1848-1852.* Translated by Janet Lloyd. Cambridge, London: Cambridge Univ. Press, 1983.

Albert, Phyllis Cohen. *The Modernization of French Jewry: Consistory and Community in the Nineteenth Century.* Hanover, New Hampshire: Brandeis Univ. Press, 1977.

Amann, Peter. "Changing Outlines of 1848," *American Historic Review*, 68 (July, 1963): 938-53.

Anderson, R. D. *Education in France, 1848-1870.* London: Clarendon, 1975.

Baker, Donald N. and Harrigan, Patrick J. *The Making of Frenchmen: Current Directions in the History of Education in France, 1679- 1979.* Waterloo: Historical Reflections, 1980.

Bédry, Marie Bernadette. "L'Instruction primaire dans l'arrondissement de Toulouse sous le Second Empire," *Annales du midi,* 91 (no. 144, 1979): 467-95.

Bellanger, Claude; Godéchot, Jacques; Guiral, Pierre, and Terrou, Fernand. *Histoire générale de la presse française.* 3 Vols. Paris: Presses Universitaires de France, 1969.

130

Bellet, Roger. *Presse et journalisme sous le Second Empire*. Paris: Colin, 1967.

Benardini, Gene. "The Origins and Development of Racial Antisemitism in Fascist Italy," *Journal of Modern History*, 49 (September 1977): 431-53.

Biddiss, Michael D. *Father of Racist Ideology: The Social and Political Thought of Count Gobineau*. New York: Weybright and Talley, 1970.

Blanchard, Pierre. *Le Vénérable Libermann, 1802-1852*. 2 Vols. Paris: Desclée de Brouver, 1960.

Bourdrel, Philippe. *Histoire des juifs de France*. Paris, A. Michel, 1974.

Brown, Marvin L. *Louis Veuillot*. Durham, North Carolina: Moore, 1977.

Busi, Frederick. *The Pope of Antisemitism, The Career and Legacy of Edouard-Adolphe Drumont*. Lanham, New York, London: University Press of America, 1986.

Byrnes, Robert F. *Antisemitism in Modern France*. New York: Howard Fertig, 1969.

Cahen, G. "Les juifs et la vie économique des campagnes (1648-1870)," *Revue d'Alsace*, 97 (1958): 141-46.

Cahuet, Alberic. *La liberté du théâtre en France et à l'étranger*. Paris: Dujarric, 1902.

Cameron, Rondo. *France and the Economic Development of Europe 1800-1914*. Princeton, N.J.: Princeton Univ. Press, 1961.

Carter, Edward C. II; Forster, Robert, and Moody, Joseph N. *Enterprise and Entrepreneurs in Nineteenth and Twentieth Century France*. Baltimore and London: John Hopkins Press, 1974.

Case, Lynn M. *French Public Opinion on War and Diplomacy during the Second Empire*. Philadelphia: Univ. of Pennsylvania Press, 1954.

Catrice, Paul. *L'harmonie entre l'église et le judaisme*. Doctoral thesis: Faculty of Lille, 1972.

Clark, Linda. *Social Darwinism in France*. University of Alabama Press, 1984.

Cohen, David, "L'image du juif dans la société française en 1843, d'après les rapports de préfets." *Revue d'Histoire économique et sociale*, (1977): 70-91.

Cohen, David. *La promotion des juifs en France à l'époque du Second Empire 1852-1870*. 2 Vols. Université de Provence: 1982.

Cohn, Jeremy. *The Friars and the Jews. The Evolution of Medieval Anti-Judaism*. Ithaca, London: Cornell Univ. Press, 1983.

Cohn Norman. *Warrant for Genocide*. New York: Harper Torchbook, 1969.

Cohn, Norman. *The Pursuit of the Millennium*, 2nd edition. New York: Harper and Row, 1961.

Daley, T. A. "Victor Séjour," *Phylon*, 4 (No.1, 1931): 5-16.

131

Dansette, Adrien. *Religious History of Modern France*. 2 Vols. Volume I. *From Revolution to the Third Republic*, translated by John Dingle. New York: Herder and Herder, 1961.

Davis, Alan T. "Religion and Racism: The Case of French Antisemitism," *Journal of Church and State*, 20 (Spring, 1978): 273-86.

D'Heilly, P. de Rivoire. "Une élection exemplaire sous le Second Empire," *Revue Administrative*, 174 (1976): 681-83.

Desdunes, Rudolphe L. *Nos hommes et notre histoire*. Montreal: Arbour and Dupont, 1911.

Duker, Abraham G. and Ben-Horin, Meir (eds.). *Emancipation and Counter-Emancipation*. New York: Ktav, 1974.

Dutacq, François. *Gustave Rouland, Ministre de l'Instruction publique. 1856-1863*. Paris: Tulle, 1910.

Elbogen, I. *A Century of Jewish Life*. Philadelphia: Jewish Publication Society, 1960.

Emden, Paul H. *Money Powers of Europe*. New York: Appleton-Century, 1938.

Feuerwerker, David. *L'émancipation des juifs en France de l'Ancien Régime à la fin de Second Empire*. Paris: Michel, 1976.

Flannery, Edward. *The Anguish of the Jews, Twenty-three Centuries of Anti-Semitism*. New York: Macmillan, 1965.

Ginsburger, Moses E. "Les familes Lehmann et Cerfberr," in *Revue des Études juives*, 49 (1910): 106-30.

Ginsburger, Moses E. "Les troubles contre les juifs d'Alsace en 1848," *Revue des Études juives*, 64 (1912): 109-17.

Girard, Louis. *La politique des travaux publics du Second Empire*. Paris: Colin, 1952.

Glasberg, Victor M. "Intent and Consequences: The Jewish Question in the French Socialist Movement of the Late Nineteenth Century," *Jewish Social Studies*, 36 (January 1974): 61-71.

Gossez, Remi. "La résistance à l'impôt les quarante-cinq centimes," *Études, Société d' Histoire de la Révolution de 1848*. Paris, 1953.

Gough, Austin. *Between Two Romes*. Oxford: Clarendon Press, 1986.

Grew, Raymond and Harrigan, Patrick J. "The Catholic Contribution to Universal Schooling in France, 1850-1906," *Journal of Modern History*, 57 (June, 1985): 211-47.

Gruau, Colonel. "Le centenaire d' Edmond About," *Nouvelle Revue*, 93 (January- February 1928): 3-12, 123-31.

Guitton, Jean. *La conversion de Ratisbonne*. Paris: Wesmael-Charlier,1964.

Gurian, Waldemar. "Louis Veuillot," *Catholic Historical Review*, 36 (January 1951): 385-414.

Hallays-Dabot, Victor. *La censure dramatique et le théâtre.* Paris, 1871.

Harrigan, Patrick J. "Social and Political Implications of Catholic Secondary Education during the Second French Empire,"*Societas*, 6-7 (Winter 1976): 41-59.

Harrigan, Patrick J. "The Church and Pluralistic Education: the Development of Teaching in French Catholic Secondary Schools, 1850-1870," *Catholic Historical Review*, 64 (April 1978): 165-213.

Harrison, J. F. C. *The Second Coming: Popular Millenarianism, 1780-1850.* New Brunswick, N. J.: Rutgers Univ. Press, 1979.

Hewit, A. F. "Ratisbonne, Alphonse, Conversion from Judaism," *Catholic World.* 39 (August 1884): 613-26.

Hoffman, Robert L. *More Than a Trial, The Struggle Over Captain Dreyfus.* New York: Free Press, London: Collier MacMillan, 1980.

Holtman, Robert B. *The Napoleonic Revolution.* Baton Rouge, London: Louisiana State Univ. Press, 1984.

Hyman, Paula. *From Dreyfus to Vichy, the Remaking of French Jewry.* NewYork: Columbia Univ. Press, 1979.

Isaac, Jules. *The Teaching of Contempt, Christian Roots of Antisemitism.* Translated by Helen Weaver. New York, Chicago, San Francisco: Holt, Rinehart and Winston, 1964.

Isaac, Jules. *L'Affaire Finaly.* Marseilles: Editions du circle intellectuel pour le rayonnement de la pensée et de la culture juive, 1953.

Isser, Natalie. *The Second Empire and the Press: A Study of Government-Inspired Brochures on French Foreign Policy in Their Propaganda Milieu.* Hague: Nijhoff, 1974.

Isser, Natalie. "The Mallet Affair: Case Study of a Scandal," *Revue des Études juives*, 137 (July-December 1979): 291-305.

Isser, Natalie. "The Linneweil Affair, A Study in Adolescent Vulnerability," *Adolescence*, 19 (Fall, 1984): 629-42.

Isser, Natalie. "The Revolution of 1848 and Human Rights: the Jews, Sweet, J. (ed.) *Proceedings of Western Society for French History*, XII, 1984, published 1986: 343-56.

Isser, Natalie and Schwartz, Lita. *A History of Conversion and Contemporary Cults.* New York, London: Peter Lang, 1988.

Isser, Natalie and Schwartz, Lita. "Sudden Conversion," *Jewish Social Studies*, 45 (Winter 1983): 17-30.

Isser, Natalie and Schwartz, Lita. "Minority Self-Hatred," *Journal of Psychology and Judaism*, 7 (Spring, Summer, 1983): 101-17.

Isser, Natalie and Schwartz, Lita. "Charismatic Leadership," *Journal of Cultic Studies*, 3 (no.1, 1986): 57-77.

Kahn-Raqbecq, N. H. "Comment le departement du Haut-Rhin devint Bonapartiste," *Revolution de 1848*, 32 (1936): 130-40.

Kann, Robert, A. "Assimilation and Antisemitism in the German-French Orbit in the Nineteenth and Early Twentieth Centuries," *Leo Baeck Institute Yearbook*, 14 (1969): 92-115.

Katz, Jacob. *Emancipation and Assimilation, Studies in Modern Jewish History*. Westmead, England: 1972.

Katz, Jacob. *Out of the Ghetto: The Social Background of Jewish Emancipation, 1770-1870*. Cambridge, Mass.: Harvard Univ. Press, 1973.

Katz, Jacob. "Religion as a Uniting and Dividing Force in Modern Jewish History," in Katz, Jacob (ed.). *The Role of Religion in Modern Jewish History*. Cambridge, Mass.: Association for Jewish Studies, 1975, 1-19.

Katz, Jacob. *From Prejudice to Destruction, Antisemitism, 1700-1933*. Cambridge, Mass.: Harvard Univ. Press, 1980.

Klein, Paul. "Mauvais, juif, mauvais chrétien," *Revue de la Pensée juive*, 17 (1951): 87-103.

Korn, Bertram M. *The American Reaction to the Mortara Case, 1858-1859*. Cincinnati: Jewish Archives, 1957.

Kselman, Thomas A. *Miracles and Prophecies in Nineteenth Century France*. New Brunswick, N. J.: Rutgers Univ. Press, 1983.

La Gorce, Pierre de. *Histoire du Second Empire*. 7 Vols. Paris, 1894-1905.

Landes, David S. "French Entrepreneurship and Industrial Growth in the 19th Century," *Journal of Economic History*, 9 (May, 1949): 45-61.

Launay, Marcel. "Le diocèse de Nantes sous le Second Empire: Monseigneur Jacquemet (1849-1869)," *Information Historique*, 44 (no. 5, 1982): 207-13.

Lazard, Raymond. *Michel Goudchaux, 1797-1862, son oeuvre et vie politique*. Paris: Alcan, 1907.

Lebrun, François. *Histoire des catholiques en France du XVe siècle à nos jours*. Toulouse: Privat, 1980.

Lecanuet, R. P. *Montalembert*. 3 Vols. Paris, 1905.

Le Clère, Bernard and Wright, Vincent. *Les préfets du Second Empire*. Paris: Colin, 1973.

Lefebvre, Georges. *Napoleon from Tilst to Waterloo, 1907-1815*. 2 Vols. Translated by J. E. Anderson. New York: Columbia Univ. Press, 1969.

Leuilliot, Paul. *L' Alsace au début du XIXe siècle: Essais d'histoire politique éco-nomique et religieuse.* 3 Vols. Paris: S. E. V. P. E. N., 1959.

Leveillant, I. "La génèse de l'antisémitisme sous la Troisème République." *Revue des Études juives,* 53 (1907): 66-89.

Lewin, Kurt. *Resolving Social Conflicts.* Translated by Gertrud Weiss Lewin. New York: Harper and Row, 1948.

L'Huillier, Fernand. "L'attitude politique de Mgr. Raess entre 1859 et 1879." *Études alsaciennes:* Société savante d'Alsace et des regions de l'Est, 1947: 245-61.

Lichtheim, George. "Socialism and the Jews," *Dissent,* 15 (July, August 1968): 314-42.

Locke, Robert E. *French Legitimists and the Politics of Moral Order in the Early Third Republic.* Princeton, N. J.,: Princeton Univ. Press, 1974.

Lovsky, E. *Antisémitisme et mystère d' Israël.* Paris: Michel, 1955.

Maccoby, Hyam. "Theologian of the Holocaust," *Commentary,* 74 (December 1982): 33-37.

Mahler, Raphael. *A History of Modern Jewry,* Vol. I, 1780-1815. New York: Shocken, 1971.

Malino, Frances and Wasserstein, Bernard. *The Jews in Modern France.* Hanover, London: Univ. of New England Press, 1985.

Margadant, Ted W. *French Peasants in Revolt, the Insurrection of 1851.* Princeton, N. J.: Princeton Univ. Press, 1979.

Marraro, Howard R. *American Opinion on the Unification of Italy.* New York: Columbia Univ. Press, 1932.

Marrus, Michael R. *The Politics of Assimilation: A Study of the French Jewish Community at the Time of the Dreyfus Affair.* Oxford: Clarendon Press, 1971.

Maurain, Jean. *Politique ecclésiastique de Second Empire.* Paris: Alcan, 1930.

Maury-Bonet. *Histoire de la liberté de conscience en France.* Paris, 1900.

Merriman, John M. *The Agony of the Republic: The Repression of the Left in Rev-olutionary France 1848-1851.* New Haven, London: Yale Univ. Press, 1978.

Moody, Joseph N. *French Education since Napoleon.* Syracuse: Syracuse Univ. Press, 1978.

Morienval, Jean. *Les créateurs de la grande presse en France: Émile de Girardin, H. de Villemessant, Moïse Millaud.* Paris: Editions Spes, 1934.

Mosse, George. *Toward the Final Solution.* New York: Fertig, 1978.

Muhlstein, Anka. *The Rise of the French Rothschilds.* New York, Paris: Vendome, 1983.

Netter, Nathan. *Vingt siècles d'histoire d'une communauté juive.* Paris: Libraire Lipschutz, 1938.

O'Neill, Charles Edward. "Theatrical Censorship in France, 1844-1875," *Harvard Library Bulletin*, 26 (October 1978): 417-41.

Papneck, Miriam Lewin. "Psychological Aspects of Minority Group Membership, the concepts of Kurt Lewin," *Jewish Social Studies*, 36 (1974): 72-79.

Phayer, J. Michael. *Sexual Liberation and Religion in Nineteenth Century Europe*. London: Croom Held, 1977.

Pierrard, Pierre. *Juifs et catholiques français*. Paris: Fayard, 1970.

Pimienta, Robert. *La propagande Bonapartiste en 1848*. Paris, 1911.

Poliakov, Léon. *History of Antisemitism*. Vol. III. *From Voltaire to Wagner*. Translated by Miriam Kochan. New York: Vanguard, 1975.

Poliakov, Léon. "Antisemitism and Christian Teaching," *Midstream*, 13 (March 1966): 13-18.

Posener, Samuel. "The Social Life of the Jewish Communities in France." *Jewish Social Studies*, 7 (1945): 195-232.

Posener, Samuel. *Adolph Crémieux*. Translated by Eugene Golob. Philadelphia: Jewish Publication Society, 1940.

Price, Roger. *The French Second Republic, A Social History*. Ithaca, New York: Cornell Univ. Press, 1972.

Rapp, Frances, et al. *Histoire des diocèses de France: Strasbourg*. Paris: Beauchesne, 1982.

Ratcliffe, Barrie M. "Crisis and Identity: Gustave d'Eichthal and Judaism in the Emancipation Period," *Jewish Social Studies*, 37 (1975): 122-40.

Ratcliffe, Barrie M. "Some Jewish Problems in the Early Careers of Emile and Isaac Pereire," *Jewish Social Studies*, 34 (1972): 189-206.

Rémond, Réné. *L'anti-cléricalisme en France de 1815 à nos jours*. Paris. Fayard, 1976.

Roth, Cecil. *A History of the Jews of Italy*. Philadelphia: Jewish Publication Society, 1976.

Ruether, Rosemary. *Faith and Fraticide*. New York: Seabury Press, 1974.

Schama, Simon. *Two Rothschilds and the Land of Israel*. New York: Knopf, 1978.

Schwarzfuchs, Simon. *Napoleon, the Jews and the Sanhedrin*. London, Boston: Routledge and Kegan, 1979.

Schwarzfuchs, Simon. *Les juifs de France*. Paris: Albin Michel, 1945.

Schwartz, Lita and Isser, Natalie. "Psychological perceptions of involuntary conversion," *Adolescence*, 14 (Summer 1979): 351-60.

Schwartz, Lita and Isser, Natalie. "Some Involuntary Conversion Tecniques," *Jewish Social Studies*, 43 (Winter 1981: 1-10.

Sharot, Stephen. *Judaism, a Sociology*. New York: Holmes and Meier, 1976.

Silberner, Edmund. "Charles Fourier on the Jewish Question," *Jewish Social Studies*, 8 (October 1946): 245-59.

Silberner, Edmund. "Pierre Leroux's Ideas on the Jewish People," *Jewish Social Studies*, 12 (1950): 367-84.

Silberner, Edmund. "French Socialism and the Jewish Question, 1865-1914," *Historica Judaica*, 15 (April 1954): 3-38.

Sobul, Albert. "La question paysanne en 1848," *La Pensée*, 18 (1948): 55-66, 19-37.

Spencer, Philip. *Politics of Belief in Nineteenth Century France: Lacordaire, Michon, Veuillot*. London: Faber and Faber, n.d.

Stadtler, Eduard. "Die Judenkrawalle von 1848 in Elsässe," *Elsässiche Monatsschrift fur Geschichte und Volkskunde*, 2 (1911): 673-86.

Stern, Fritz. *Gold and Iron, Bismarck, Bleichröder, and the Building of the German Empire*. New York: Knopf, 1977.

Szajkowski, Zosa. "Simon Deutz: Traitor or French Patriot?" *Jewish Social Studies*, 16 (1965): 53-67.

Szajkowski, Zosa. "The Schools of the Alliance Israelite Universelle," *Historia Judaica*, 22 (April, 1960): 3-22.

Szajkowski, Zosa. *Poverty and Social Welfare Among French Jews 1800-1880*. New York, 1954.

Szajkowski, Zosa. *Jewish Education in France 1789-1939*. New York: Columbia Univ. Press, 1956.

Szajkowski, Zosa. "The Jewish Saint-Simonians and Socialist Antisemitism in France," *Jewish Social Studies*, 9 (1947): 33-60.

Terdiman, Richard. *Discourse, Counter Discourse*. Ithaca: Cornell Univ. Press, 1985.

Thiébaut, Marcel. *Edmond About*. Paris: Galliard, 1936.

Tinker, Edward Larocque. *Les écrits de langue française en Louisiane au XIXe siècle*. Reprint, Wendeln Kraus, 1970.

Toynbee, Arnold. *A Study of History*. An abridgement of Vols. I-IV by D. C. Somervill. New York, London: Oxford Univ. Press, 1947.

Trachtenberg, Joshua. *The Devil and the Jews*. Cleveland, New York, Philadelphia: Meridian Books, 1943.

Valentin, Hugo. *Antisemitism: Historically and Critically Examined*. Translated by A. G. Chater. New York: Viking Press, 1936.

Vaux, G. and Riondel, Henri. *Vie du Père Jean Roothan, 1785-1853*. Paris: Lethielleux, 1935.

Volli, Gemma. *Il casa Mortara nel primo centenario*. Rome: La Rassegna Mensile di Israel, 1960.

Weber, Eugen. *Peasants into Frenchmen: the Modernization of Rural France 1870-1914.* Stanford, Ca.: Stanford Univ. Press, 1976.

Weil, A. "Un precedent de l'Affaire Mortara," *Revue Historique* (May 1921): 49-65.

Weill, Georges. "Les Saint-Simoniens sous Napoléon III," *Revue des Études napoleoniennes,* I (1912): 391-406.

Wilson, Stephen. *Ideology and Experience: Antisemitism in France at the Time of the Dreyfus Affair.* Rutherford, N. J.: Fairleigh Dickinson Univ. Press, 1982.

Wistrich, Robert J. *Revolutionary Jews from Marx to Trotsky.* London, New York: Barnes and Noble, 1976.

Zeldin, Theodore. *France: 1848-1945.* 2 Vols. Oxford: Oxford Univ. Press, 1973-1977.

Zeldin, Theodore (ed.). *Conflicts in French Society.* London: 1970.

Zind, Pierre. *L'ensieignement religieux dans l'instruction primaire publique en France de 1850 à 1873.* Lyon: Centre historique de Catholicisme, 1976.

Index

146